AF819355

APPROAC
AND I

Approaches To Training And Development

Niranjan Kaur Sardar

MANGLAM

MANGLAM PUBLICATIONS
DELHI-110053 (INDIA)

Published by :

MANGLAM PUBLICATIONS

L-21/1, Street No. 5, Shivaji Marg, Near Kali Mandir,
J.P. Nagar, Kartar Nagar, West Ghonda, Delhi-110053
Phone : 011-22945677, (M.) 9968367559, 9868572512
E-mail: manglam.books2007@rediffmail.com
manglam.publications2007@rediffmail.com

Approaches To Training and Development

© Reserved

First Edition 2010

ISBN 978-93-80013-50-3

All rights reserved no part of this work may be reproduced, stored in a retrieval system, or transmitted in any form or by any means, electronic, mechanical, photocopying, recording or otherwise, without the prior written permission of the Publisher.

PRINTED IN INDIA

Published by Ravindra Kumar Yadav for Manglam Publications, Delhi-110053 Laser Typeset by Sai Graphics, Delhi- 110002, Printed at Sachin Printers, Moujpur Delhi- 53

Preface

The concept of training has recently become a strategic option in the development of human resources. Consequently, the strategies of development which aim at improving, modernizing and simplifying work methods have been greatly required as a pressing need in all governmental bodies. The modern concept of training provides that training should convey the basic theoretical and practical skills in a way that copes with the latest challenges represented in the ever changing work requirements.

A greater emphasis on 'learning' as opposed to 'training'. This isnot simply a pedantic difference but is a sea change indicating a major movement from the role of the trainer to that of the learner in a training programme. 'Training' stems from the trainer who, in being the principal in a programme, has the expectation that the participants will learn as a result of the messages being passed to them. 'Learning' is the internal action and result for the participants and places learning activities firmly where they belong - in the hands of the learners themselves, aided and supported by the trainer. Achange in role for many trainers from the 'stand at the front of the group and tell them' approach to one where they have a multi-role as both providers of learning resources (sometimes, but notalways, in the form of their input sessions), and facilitators helping the learners in their learning achievements. Even when trainer inputs are necessary, these will be completely different from the simple 'talk and chalk' approach, using all the modern trainingaids available. A developing involvement in training and development of electronicmethods of knowledge dissemination and aids to skill development.These include the CD-ROM, the interactive CD-ROM, Internet training programme provision and the increasing use of in-company Intranet.

The Training and Development Department exerts utmost efforts to develop training programs through application of the most advanced techniques in training to confront recent challenges and developments at work environment and bridge the gap between actual and targeted levels of performance, through qualified lecturers who maintain required theoretical and practical skills. There is no doubt that the construction of a solid base of administrators and trainers has become the fruitful outcome of dedicated efforts over the past years of continued training and development

N.K. Sardar

Contents

1

Importance of Systematic Approaches to Training

Many of us assume that we already have good training for ourselves and our employees After all, we answer our employees' questions as they have them. We send our employees to a course once in a while. Sure, our approach to training isn't intentional, that is, planned and focused. But our employees seem to be doing their jobs without have any real problems.

Unfortunately, we don't know what we don't know. It may be that our employees could be performing much better than we realize if they had better skills. It might be that we supervisors could get back a lot of time that otherwise is spent answering our employees' questions. We might retain our employees much longer, as well. Addressing this possibility. isn't a "what if question, it's a primary responsibility of a supervisor.

Adopting a systematic approach to training helps ensure that supervisors are getting the most out of themselves and their employees. A systematic approach to training includes taking the time to analyze what results the organization needs from its employees, if employees are accomplishing those results, and what training and development approaches are needed by employees to better accomplish those results. A systematic approach includes evaluating approaches before, during and after training to ensure employees truly benefited from the training in terms of enhanced results to the organization.

Effective training and development includes using sound principles of performance management and good, basic training techniques.

Basic Overview of Some Systematic Approaches to Training

The following manuals outline systematic training processes. A systems approach ensures a comprehensive training process that remains focused on the needs of the organization. The process typically includes the phases.

Analyze the organization's needs and identify training goals which, when reached, will equip learner's with knowledge and skills to meet the organization's needs. Usually this phase also includes identifying when training should occur and who should attend as learners.

Design a training system that learners and trainers can implement to meet the learning goals; typically includes identifying learning objectives (which culminate in reaching the learning goals), needed facilities, necessary funding, course content, lessons and sequence of lessons.

Develop a training "package" of resources and materials, including, e.g., developing audio visuals, graphics, manuals, etc.

Implement the training package, including delivering the training, support group feedback, clarifying training materials, administering tests and conducting the final evaluation. This phase can include administrative activities, such as copying, scheduling facilities, taking attendance data, billing learners, etc.

Evaluate training, including before, during and after implementation of training.

In a systematic approach to training, each phase of the process produces results needed by the next phase. For example, the training analysis phase produces learning goals that are used by the next phase, training design. Training design (often called instructional design) references the goals to design methods and materials from which learners can reach the goals and objectives. Typically, each phase provides ongoing evaluation feedback to other phases in order to improve the overall systems process.

Similarity Between Systematic Training Process and Performance Management Process

Readers who have read Performance Management. An Overview in this library will note the similarity between the processes of systematic training and performance management. The results from implementing the two processes are highly integrated as well. That's why if a supervisor uses good principles of performance management then training and development can be a straightforward activity which almost always contribute to the organization's bottom line.

The performance management process is repeated below from the library section, Performance Management. When reviewing the steps below, think of the word "domain" as applying to the employee being trained. Comments are added in italics. The words "employee" and "learner" are used interchangeably.

Review organizational goals to associate preferred organizational results in terms of units of performance, that is, quantity, quality, cost or timeliness (note that the result itself is therefore a measure) Reviewing these goals will prepare the supervisor and employee for soon ensuring that training produces useful results for the organization.

Implementing a good training plan will produce results for the organization. Specify desired results for the domain – as guidance, focus on results needed by other domains (e.g., products or services need by internal or external customers) The training process should have specific learning goals to accomplish which, in turn, help the learner accomplish specific results.

Ensure the domain's desired results directly contribute to the organization's result – A good training plan must be geared to help the employee produce specific results, which in turn, directly contribute to results needed by the organization

Weight, or prioritize, the domain's desired results Knowing what range of results are needed from the employee and which are the most important, helps the supervisor and employee to pick what training is needed and when.

Identify first level measures to evaluate if and how well the domain's desired results were achieved This refinement of expected results from the employee helps the supervisor and employee to ensure that training is highly focused on results for the employee and organization. this step is similar to setting standards against which the training will be evaluated Identify more specific measures for each first level measure if necessary. This step is similar to setting up front training goals in the training plan, and associating measures from which the effectiveness of training can later be evaluated. Identify standards for evaluating how well the desired results were achieved e.g., "below expectations, "meets expectations" and "exceeds expectations Document a performance plan including desired results, measures and standards. This is similar to developing the training plan, with preferred training goals and measures.

Conduct ongoing observations and measurements to track performance The training plan is implemented and includes ongoing evaluation before, during and after carrying out training methods.

Exchange ongoing feedback about performance Effective training requires ongoing feedback between learners and trainer. Conduct a performance appraisal (sometimes called performance review). Effective training includes evaluation to judge the quality of the training itself and identify what results were achieved by learners.

If performance meets the desired performance standard, then reward for performance (the nature of the reward depends on the domain) Hopefully, the learning experience includes time to acknowledge successes and the trainers' and learners' roles in those successes. If performance does not meet performance standards, develop or update a performance development plan A good training plan will include measures for noting changes in the employee's performance. If improvement is needed, a performance plan should be updated or started, and may include cause for more training. Likewise, the trainer should review results of learners' evaluations to improve the quality of his or her training design.

2

The Competency Based Approach to Training

Throughout the world, millions of students go to school every day. These students study subjects such as science, language and mathematics in courses usually scheduled to last the duration of the school year. Because progression through the various subjects in school is time based, at any given time during the year the teacher is expected to be at a specific point in the textbook or course content. While not every student may progress at the same rate, the schedule typically requires everyone to move at the same rate as the teacher. Tests are administered periodically to ensure students understand the concepts and principles. Test scores often are compared to determine the grades of the students. Unfortunately, when a student does not do well on a test there often is little time for individual assistance as the teacher must move on in order to adhere to the established time schedule.

While traditional, time based approaches to education have met with varying levels of success over the years, it is an ineffective system when the goal is to train individuals to perform specific, job related skills. For example, an active, certified airline pilot is attending a 3 week training course to learn to fly a new type of aircraft. Will attending all sessions during the course, ensure the pilot can fly the plane.

Of course not! If the pilot is unable to attend 2 days of the course, does this mean the pilot cannot fly the plane. Probably not. After 4 days, the pilot does poorly on a written test.

Should the pilot immediately fail the course or should the pilot continue with assistance and be given the opportunity to be tested again. If the pilot can pass all written tests does this indicate that the pilot can fly the plane. No! In addition to assessing knowledge, an evaluation of the pilot's skills also is required. Obviously, the time based educational system used in schools and universities is not appropriate when conducting training. A more appropriate approach is competency based training (CBT).

What is CBT.

In a traditional educational system, the unit of progression is time and it is teacher centered. In a CBT system, the unit of progression is mastery of specific knowledge and skills and is learner or participantcentered. Two key terms used in competency based training are.

- Skill—A task or group of tasks performed to a specific level of competency or proficiency which often use motor functions and typically require the manipulation of instruments and equipment. Some skills, however, such as counseling, are knowledge and attitudebased.
- Competency—A skill performed to a specific standard under specific conditions.

There appears to be substantial support for competency based training. Norton (1987) believes that competency based training should be used as opposed to the "medieval concept of time based learning." Foyster (1990) argues that using the traditional "school" model for training is inefficient.

After in depth examinations of three competencybased programs, Anthony Watson (1990) concluded that competency based instruction has tremendous potential for training in industry. Moreover, in a 1990 study of basic skills education programs in business and industry, Paul Delker found that successful training programs were competency based.

A competent clinician e.g., physician, nurse, midwife, medical assistant) is one who is able to perform a clinical skill to a satisfactory standard. Competencybased training for reproductive health professionals then is training based upon the participant's ability to demonstrate attainment or mastery of clinical skills performed under certain conditions to specific standards (the skills then become competencies). Norton describes five essential elements of a CBT system.

- Competencies to be achieved are carefully identified, verified and made public in advance.
- Criteria to be used in assessing achievement and the conditions under which achievement will be assessed are explicitly stated and made public in advance.
- The instructional program provides for the individual development and evaluation of each of the competencies specified.
- Assessment of competency takes the participant's knowledge and attitudes into account but requires actual performance of the competency as the primary source of evidence.
- Participants progress through the instructional program at their own rate by demonstrating the attainment of the specified competencies.

Characteristics of CBT

How does one identify a competency based training program. In addition to a set of competencies, what other characteristics are associated with CBT. According to Foyster (1990), Delker (1990) and Norton (1987) there are a number of characteristics of competency based programs.

Advantages and Limitations of CBT

One of the primary advantages of CBT is that the focus is on the success of each participant. Watson (1990) states that the competency based approach "appears especially useful in training situations where trainees have to attain a small number of specific and job related competencies". Benefits of CBT identified by Norton (1987) include.

- Participants will achieve competencies required in the performance of their jobs.
- Participants build confidence as they succeed in mastering specific competencies.
- Participants receive a transcript or list of the competencies they have achieved.
- Training time is used more efficiently and effectively as the trainer is a facilitator of learning as opposed to a provider of information.
- More training time is devoted to working with participants individually or in small groups as opposed to presenting lectures.
- More training time is devoted to evaluating each participant's ability to perform essential job skills. While there are a number of advantages of competency based training, there also are some potential limitations. Prior to implementing CBT, it is important to consider these limitations.

- Unless initial training and followup assistance is provided for the trainers, there is a tendency to "teach as we were taught" and CBT trainers quickly slip back into the role of the traditional teacher.
- A CBT course is only as effective as the process used to identify the competencies. When little or no attention is given to identification of the essential job skills, then the resulting training course is likely to be ineffective.
- A course may be classified as competencybased, but unless specific CBT materials and training approaches (e.g., learning guides, checklists and coaching) are designed to be used as part of a CBT approach, it is unlikely that the resulting course will be truly competency based.

Models and Simulations in CBT

Models and simulations are used extensively in competency based training courses. Airplane pilots first learn to fly in a simulator. Supervisors first learn to provide feedback to employees using role plays during training. Individuals learning to administer cardiopulmonary resuscitation (CPR) practice this procedure on a model of a human mannequin.

Satur and Gupta (1994) developed a model which facilitates skill development in performing and evaluating coronary anastomoses with an angioscope. The results of their study indicate that models are proving invaluable as a training tool. George H. Buck in a 1991 historical review of the use of simulators in medical education concluded that "Given the developments in this technology within the last 50 years, it is possible that the use of simulators will increase in the future, should the need arise to teach new concepts and procedures at set times to large groups of individuals". Researchers in two different experimental studies involving training people to perform breast self examinations compared several methods and found that using models was the most effective training method Campbell et. al., 1991 and Assaf et. al., 1985. In a multicenter evaluation of training of physicians in the use of 30 cm flexible sigmoidoscopy, Weissman et al (1987) found that they were easily trained by first practicing on plastic colon models.

Norton believes that participants in a competency based training course should learn in an environment that duplicates or simulates the work place. Richards (1985) in writing about performance testing indicates that assessment of skills requires tests using simulations e.g., models and role plays) or work samples i.e., performing actual tasks under controlled conditions in either a laboratory or a job setting). Finally, Delker in a study of business and industry found that the best approach for training involved learner centered instruction using print, instructional technology and simulations.

Evaluation and Assessment in CBT

Evaluation in traditional courses typically involves administering knowledge based tests. While knowledge based assessments can certainly be used in CBT to measure mastery of information, the primary focus is on measuring mastery of skills. In keeping with this, Thomson reports that the decision to recognize a performance as satisfactory and to determine competence should be the basis for success of a competency based program. Moreover, Foyster argues that assessment in competency based programs must be criterion referenced with the criterion being the competencies upon which the program is based. Finally, Richards indicates that simulation and work sample performance tests should include a checklist or some type of rating scale.

Implications for Using CBT

In a 1990 study of three operating competency based programs, Anthony Watson identified a number of implications for organizations considering implementing a CBT system.

- Organizations must be committed to providing adequate resources and training materials.
- Audiovisual materials need to be directly related to the written materials.
- Training activities need to match the objectives.
- Continuous participant interaction and feedback must take place.
- Trainers must be trained to conduct competency based training courses.
- Individuals attending training must be prepared for CBT as this approach is likely to be very different from their past educational and training experiences.

JHPIEGO's Approach to CBT

JHPIEGO Corporation has adopted a competencybased approach to conducting clinical training in selected reproductive health practices. Based on the principles summarized in this paper, JHPIEGO's approach to CBT involves key activities which occur during the design, delivery and evaluation of training courses. These activities are summarized here and explained in detail in JHPIEGO's Clinical Training Skills for Reproductive Health Professionals and Advanced Training Skills for Reproductive Health Professionals reference manuals. The key activities around which JHPIEGO's competency based training is built include design, delivery and evaluation activities.

Transfer of Training

JHPIEGO uses a four step process to transfer specific clinical skills and knowledge from experts to service providers. These steps are part of the process of developing a family planning training system within a country. The four steps include.

- Standardizing provision of clinical services and modifying and adapting JHPIEGO training materials as necessary
- Training service providers to provide these services competently, according to the approved standards
- Identifying and preparing proficient service providers to function as clinical skill trainers so they are able to train other service providers
- Identifying and preparing clinical skill trainers to function as advanced and eventually master trainers so that they are able to train other clinical skill trainers, evaluate training and develop or revise course materials

The first step is to standardize the clinical skill(s) to be used in the delivery of family planning services. For example, in a country there may be a need to train clinicians to perform IUD insertions and removals. The first activity conducted is to identify and observe a group of clinicians who are performing these procedures. The steps the clinicians perform are observed and compared to the standard approach outlined in JHPIEGO's competency based IUD learning guides and checklists. This observation process gives JHPIEGO trainers an idea of the skill levels of those skills. The clinical skills course is based on a training package consisting of a reference manual, supporting audiovisuals, anatomic models, and trainer and participant handbooks (which contain the learning guides and checklists based on the standardized procedure). Following the clinical skills course, these competent service providers provide clinical services to clients. After providing services for a period of time, a group of the most proficient service providers who have demonstrated an interest and who will be trained to be service providers. As necessary, JHPIEGO's learning guides and checklists are modified to meet the specific service delivery standards or norms within the host country. The standardized procedure then forms the basis for the service provider training courses conducted within the country.

The second step is to train a specific group of service providers to perform the standardized clinical willingness to become clinical trainers undergo training skills training.

The third step in the transfer process is to prepare a group of proficient service providers to be clinical skill trainers. These service providers attend a clinical training skills course which also is based on a training package. During this course, participants will have their clinical knowledge updated and skills assessed and standardized to ensure they are proficient at performing the clinical skill. Participants will then learn how to demonstrate clinical skills, transfer knowledge and skills during training, function as clinical coaches, and use competency based learning guides and checklists to assess participant performance. Following the clinical training skills course these clinical skill trainers conduct service provider training courses.

During their first service provider course they either co train with an advanced or master clinical trainer or are observed by a training skills trainer. The final step in the process of transferring skills is to prepare a small group of proficient clinical skill trainers to become advanced trainers. These clinical skill trainers attend an advanced training skills course which is also based on a training package. During this course, participants learn how to conduct needs assessments, design training courses, facilitate the group dynamics occurring during a course, and evaluate training.

Following the advanced training skills course these advanced trainers conduct clinical training skills courses. During their first several training courses they cotrain with a master trainer. After successfully delivering several training skills courses these individuals can be qualified to function as a master trainer.

Based on the concepts and principles presented in this paper, the key features of JHPIEGO's approach to training include.

- Development of competencies (knowledge, attitude and practice) is based on national standards.
- Quality of performance is built into the training process.
- Emphasis of the training is on development of qualified providers, not on the number of clinicians undergoing training.
- Training builds competency and confidence because participants know what level of performance is expected, how knowledge and skills will be evaluated, that progression through training is self paced, and that there are opportunities for practice until mastery is achieved.

Approach to Training Extension Personnel

One of the important mandate of the KVK is to organize training programmes for inservice grass root level extension personnel. In this section therefore, approach to training of extension personnel has been dealt briefly. There are mainly three models of training. These are. i) discrete phases or traditional model, ii) interdependent and interrelated process model; and iii) system model.

The Discrete Phases Model is most frequently used training model consists of five discrete phases connected sequentially; assessment, objective setting, design, implementation and evaluation. Each phase stands independently of the other phases. It has several consequences;

(i) needs assessment data are prematurely organized and stated as training needs which results in;

(ii) objectives stated in very general and unmeasurable terms and not closely related to the real training needs which leads to;

(iii) programmes designed and implemented which are only slightly related to the real training needs or "real life" circumstances faced by trainees. In general, this model of training leads to increasingly more general and less precise training efforts.

The Interdependent and Interrelated Process Model is used in which the five phases form sub processes which are highly interrelated and interdependent on all other subprocesses as well as on the total process.

The Systems Model is a problem solving process that places the diagnosis of needs before the presentation of methods required to achieve the needs. It is a discipline that requires those responsible for designing and providing the training that people need to carry out a series of interdependent steps in a logical sequence. The details of this model follow as it is suited to KVK in service training. The System Model consists of a number of subsystems which are interdependent.

The System model is a diagnostic approach. It diagnoses the performance problem. It prescribes remedy only after a careful diagnosis of the problem. It develops the training systems in five distinct and sequential phases of development. For developing a training system model, each phase is described here briefly.

Phase 1. Training Needs Assessment

This phase starts by first posing the basic question. What is the performance problem. If the answer is the gap between the desirable and the actual job performance by extension personnel, it asks the next question; what is this gap which is required to be overcome by training. In other word, what are the training needs of extension personnel. The training needs are assessed as objectively as possible, drawing a clear distinction between 'actual' and 'imagined' needs of extension personnel.

Training needs should be assessed at three levels namely,

- Individual
- Groups
- Organizational.

A number of methods for training needs assessment are available for different levels. The training needs have to be assessed within the ambit of national priorities and programmes and farmers' felt needs for training. It is essential to realize that farmers' felt needs for training lay the foundation upon which the training needs of extension personnel are required to be assessed.

Phase II. Training Plans Development

After assessment of training needs appropriate training plans are required to be developed on the basis of assessed training needs of extension personnel. A training plans can be (a) short term, (b) long term, or both. While an Annual Training Plan is an essential requirement of sound training arrangement it is desirable that training plans are develop in, say, a five year framework. The advantage of developing training plans in a 5 year framework is that management will have a reduced task of undertaking an annual review only, enabling it to devote more time to other aspects of training management, which will enhance the value of training.

Phase III. Design of Training Programmes.

In the third phase, appropriate training programmes are required to be designed after training needs assessment (Phase I) and in accordance with the developed training plans (Phase II). The starting point in the design of the training programme is a statement of its objectives. The objectives should be stated clearly and in simple, straight forward language. The use of jargon should be avoided. The objectives, not more than 3 or 5 in number, should clearly state the **Knowledge, Skills, and Attitudes** the trainee will acquired after the training and how will it be **useful** to the trainee in his job performance. The statement of objectives should enable the trainee to have a clear idea about the relevance of training programme to his training needs.

The next step is the determination of an appropriate mix of various skills required by extension personnel. Broadly, extension personnel require three types of skills, namely, i) technical, ii) human and iii) conceptual. The mix of these skills will be different for different levels of extension personnel. Weights can be attached to different skills for determination of mix. For example, the mix for Village Extension Workers can be upto 50 percent technical skills, 40 percent human skills and 10 per cent conceptual skills. Appropriate curriculum then can be developed by following the Concentric Circles Approach to Curriculum. Under this approach there are three concentric circles, the inner circle of what must be known, the middle circle of what should be known, and the outer circle of what could be known. It is imperative that the curriculum concentrates upon the inner circle of what must be known and does not drift to the outer circle of what could be known, as it very often happens in practice.

The selection of an appropriate training methods is the next step in the design of a training programme. An array training methods are available suited to different levels of extension personnel. As a general rule, a mix of training methods is preferable to only one training method, and the entire programme must have a problem solving practical orientation. Practical assignments and providing adequate opportunities to trainees for interaction will enhance the utility of and receptivity of training. Training technology now offers a number of training aids which can increase and reinforce learning. These include a number of visual aids (like chalkboard, flip chart, plastic writing board, magnetic board, flannel board and overhead projector), and projected aids (like slides, film strips, slide projectors, and video tapes). In addition to audio visual aids, computers are also emerging as a powerful training aid. Suffice it to say that a variety of training aids are required to be used in a training programme which will sustain the interest of trainees in message receptivity. With a view to make training an enduring exercise, supporting training material is also required to be developed simultaneously with a training programme or separately as a training input. In the former category fall lecture notes, supporting leaflets and bulletins, and as it usually the case, a compilation of course material. In the latter category fall specially developed training manuals and handbooks which can either be used in a training course or used separately by trainees on their own.

Phase IV. Training Programme Implementation

In the fourth phase, the training programmes are implemented. The implementation of training programmes is the responsibility of KVK, or more precisely, the Course Instructor. Many training programmes flounder due to poor implementation which usually reflects lack of/or inadequate preparation. Use of checklist and alertness to respond to an emergency (like non appearance of resource person in time) can prevent occurrence of many avoidable mishaps. A wise word of counsel is not to take anything for granted and to personally ensure that things are in order.

Phase V. Training Monitoring and Evaluation

In this last phase, training is monitored and evaluated. Training monitoring is relatively greater practical importance than training evaluation. Training monitoring should take place through well developed training monitoring indices like number of training courses planned and held every month and number of trainees planned and covered. The training monitoring indices will differ from level to level. These indices should be regularly brought to the notice of top management so that it can intervene to correct a situation. An evaluation of training by trainers and trainees followed by an annual review by the top management can considerably enhance the usefulness of training courses. Suitable changes in the training approach can be made as and when necessary, on the results of training monitoring and evaluation. Evaluation should be done by the course instructor with a questionnaire having questions/items related to the coverage of the content methodology of training, audio visual aids quality, stay arrangement, and communication eliciting responses from the trainees at the end of the training session/course. Such responses should be analyzed for making further improvement.

3

Human Resource Development Training and Skill Development

Development of Training Strategy–Trainair Methodology

Human Resource is the backbone of any organization. Properly trained and highly skilled human resource is perceived as the greatest asset of an organization. Skilled personnel contribute to efficiency, growth, increased productivity and market reputation of an organization.This has been realized by industrial, commericial, researach establishments and even governments. Invariably, a separate Human Resouces Development department exists in all these organizations to attend to the matters relating to recruitment, training and deployment. Technological advancements in various fields world over are very rapid, and the every other day we see new products or machines or equipments with more and more advanced features, with which users have to be acquainted. In order to cope with the industry demand and technological advancements, we need to develop training strategy for our human capital to attain the required skill levels.

Training is referred to as a method to give the new entrant or an existing employee the skills, knowledge and attitude needed to perform the job. Training should meet two basic objectives.

1. Training should make the personnel skilled enough to do the job on hand efficiently leading to targeted productivity levels.

2. Training should be cost effective.

Training must be based on scientific approach and quality training material to meet objective number one. The training duration should be as short as possible and resources used efficiently for meeting objective number 2. In this connection, I would like to describe about a training approach, called ICAO TRAINAIR Methodology, which is accepted and followed by many Civil Aviation Training establishments all over the world. The TRAINAIR is a programme of the International Civil Aviation Organization that was evolved to strengthen the basic civil aviation concept of safety and and regularity of air transport operations, by means of a high standard of training for aviation personnel through what are known as Standardized Training Packages (STPs).

The TRAINAIR course development methodology is a scientific approach of developing training courses for a job oriented objective. This methodology has both the process standard and product standard. Process standard means the standard in which the process is important but no weightage is given to the end result. Product standard means the standard in which end result is important but no weightage is given to the process. TRAINAIR methodology has both process and product standards. This methodology seeks to impart skill, knowledge and attitude required to perform the job and eliminate all things which are extraneous and not required to perform that job. That means the trainees are taught only the "Need to Know Things" and not the "Nice to Know Things". Because of this, training becomes focussed and the training time and costs, and duration of absence of the workforce from the operational units are minimized.

The TRAINAIR Standardized Training Package (STP) preparation methodology is based on an engineering approach called the system approach. It consists of following three activities.

1. Analysis
2. Design and production
3. Evaluation

All these activities are divided into 9 Phases.

Phase 1. Preliminary analysis, is invoked when a decision is to be taken whether or not training is needed to do a job on hand; then assistance of a qualified Course Developers team is requested. The course developers team visits the operational unit, analyzes the system and interviews the personnel working. The result of analysis is one of the following.

1. Recommending non training management solutions like developing a job aid such as checklists, flow charts or automation etc.
2. Develop a Standard Training Package (STP) as a training solution If it is found appropriate to proceed with a training solution by development of an STP, the Phase 2 activities commence.

In Phase 2. Job analysis, again the Course Developers team visits operational unit, interviews the working experts. The job is divided into duties, duties are divided into tasks, tasks are divided into sub tasks, and further the skill/ knowledge attitude required to carryout sub tasks are decided.

In the Phase 3. Population Analysis, the data on target

population's (i.e., intended trainee group) acquired skill/ knowledge attitude, qualifications, job experience, social background, learning preferences are collected and analyzed.

In Phase 4. Design of Curriculum, the difference in skill knowledge attitude required (decided in phase 2) and those acquired (decided in phase 3) will become the Course Curriculum. The modules and sequence of training program are decided in this phase.

In Phase 5. Design of modules, all the course materials such as Trainee Handouts, Instructor guide, Practical exercise sheets, Progress tests, key to progress tests, Mastery tests, key to mastery tests will be developed.

In Phase 6. Production and developmental testing, the prepared Mastery tests, Progress tests and practical exercises are tried out as developmental testing to check the accuracy and reliability of training materials. Detailed lesson plans to guide the instructors, hand outs for the trainees, audio visual materials etc are all prepared ready for the initial Validation delivery of the package.

In Phase 7. Validation and Revision, for the first time, the prepared course material will be tried on a group of trainees for whom the course is designed. The group of Course Developers will monitor the delivery of the course throughout, and observe the reactions of trainees and instructors. They also take a note of the result at the end of the course. If 80% of the participants passes with 80% marks or attain the standard, then the same course will be administered to the remaining trainee population in subsequent sessions. Any deficiencies noted will be corrected during this phase. At the end of this phase, all the developed training materials will be sent to the ICAO TRAINAIR Central Unit, Montreal for accord of approval as full fledged STP.

In Phase 8. Implementation, full STP Course is available for future deliveries. The same course is also available for global sharing among the members of TRAINAIR programme.

In Phase 9. Post training evaluation, the effectiveness of the course which is now implemented is evaluated by analyzing

1. Was there the desired improvement of the trainees' performance when they return to their jobs.
2. Did the training program effectively meet the operational need which gave rise to it..

This is done by gathering information which is used to make improvement in the training and determine the costs and benefits of the training development project. During the entire process of course of development, Course Developers interact with the Subject Matter Experts and skilled job performers as and when required and get the required inputs.

Conclusion

Trainer methodology guides the development of training materials in a standardized and systematic manner making it practical for course material to be shared between the Trainer programme participating Institutes. This facilitates international cooperation in training development, ensures common standards and promotes mutual confidence in the quality of the products. TRAINAIR training methodology has been found to be greatly suiting the fast growing aviation field for sustaining safe and regular air transport operatons.

Training and Development. Village Health Guides (VHG) Scheme.

The Village Health Guide Scheme was initially started as Community Health Workers' Scheme on 2nd October,

1977 in all the States except Arunachal Pradesh, J & K, Kerala and Tamil Nadu. The Scheme was renamed as Village Health Guide Scheme in 1981 when it was made 100% centrally sponsored scheme under Family Welfare Programme. According to the scheme the village community selects a volunteer as Village Health Guide who after training acts as a link between the community and the governmental health system. At present about 3.23 lakh VHGs are reported to be working. Each VHG is paid an honorarium of Rs. 50 per month. The Scheme has been reviewed by a committee of experts. The report of the committee after obtaining the comments of other relevent Min. Deptt. being forwarded to the cabinet for final decision.

Basic Training of ANM/MPHW

It is a 100% centrally sponsored scheme under Family Welfare Programme. Female Health Workers' basic training course is of 1 ½ Years duration and eligibility for admission is X class pass. The course is recognised by Indian Nursing Council. There are 478 ANM, MPW(F) Training Centres functioning in the country. These include training centres run by Voluntary Organisations with their own resources.The finnacial assistance increased w.e.f. 7.2.2001, for stipend for the trainees from 125 per month per trainee to Rs 500 per month per trainee, contingency from Rs 5000/ per annum to Rs 10000 per annum & rent for school and hostel if in rented building from Rs 2500 per annum to Rs 60,000 per annum.

Training of Multipurpose Health Worker (Male)/MPHW

It is a 100% Centrally Sponsored Scheme. Basic training is for one year and eligibility for admission is X pass. On successful completion of the training the Health Worker (M) are eligible for posting at a Sub Centre. There are 56 MPW (M) Training Centres functioning in the country as on 30.06.00. Of these, 28 training centres are functioning in Health and Family Welfare Training Centres and 28 are independent basic training schools.The financial assistance have been revised w.e.f. 7.2.2001 as follows.

Promotional Training Course for MPHW(F)

ANMs with at least 5 years of service are deputed for 6 months Promotional Training Course. After the training, they become eligible for the post of LHVs, HA(F). During the training period, the ANM is paid a stipend of Rs.150/ p.m. An LHV provides supportive supervision and technical guidance to Female Health Workers (ANMs) of 6 Sub Centres. There are 42 LHV Promotional Training Centres in the country.The pattern of financial assistance for this programme also has been revised as mentioned under the programme of basic training of ANM.

Health and Family Welfare Training Centers

Health and Family Welfare Training Centres have been established in the country with the objective to improve the quality of services by providing in service orientation training to the Medical and Para Medical personnel engaged in the delivery of Health and Family Welfare Services. There are 47 Health and Family Welfare Training Centres functioning in the country. These training centres are funded by the Department of Family Welfare, Government of India.The financial assistance for this programme has been revised as follows .

Rural Health Training Centre, Najafgarh

RHTC, Najafgarh was estblished as a Najafgarh Health Institute with the assistance of Rockfeller Foundation in 1937 and emerged as a Rural Health Training Centre in 1969. It has been rendering various services to the rural community training to medical and para medical health workers and nursing personnel from different Nursing Training Schools of Delhi, orientation training to Public

Health Students and ANMs, training of ANMs (10 + 2) Vocational Course under Central Board of Secondary Education.

Family Welfare Training Research Centre, Mumbai

Family Weflare Training and Research Centre(FWTRC), Mumbai was the first Family Planning Training Centre, established in June 1957 and was made responsible for the training needs of State and District level categories of health personnel from Western Zone. This centre has been recognised as an institution for training of central health service officers in the areas of National Family Welfare Programme and National Health Policy. FWT&RC is also conducting community based Research Projects in the field of Health and Family Welfare. The institute also conducts a one year diploma in health education (DHE).

Gandhigram Institute of Rural Health and Family Welfare Trust (GIRHFWT), Gandhigram,

To train the teachers of ANM LHV Training Schools and Public Health nurses during the Sixth Plan Period, Government of India established training institutions at Tamil Nadu (Gandhigram). The Gandhigram institution is also functioning as one of the Central Training Institutions in India to provide training to functionaries of Health and Family Welfare of Kerala, Karnataka, Pondicherry, A&N Islands as well as Tamil Nadu. The institute also conducts regular Diploma in Health Education Course of one year.

4

Academic Administrators and Higher Education in Training and Development

Higher Education institutions today face intense competitive pressures. They are required to meet increased expectations of different stake holders. These are no more insulated from the socio economic environment, where they exist, but are part of the same and are expected to play an important role in regional and national development. In this background, the academic administrators today are facing new challenges. With a view to enable them face these challenges competently, there is a need to build their capacity through structural training and development programmes. The importance of this was realized in the National Policy on Education, 1986 and Programme of Action, 1992. However, no organized efforts have been made in this direction so far. It is in this background that this scheme is being launched by the University Grants Commission.

The guidelines under the scheme lay down a broad framework for training and development of academic administrators in the universities and colleges throughout the country in a structured manner. The activity shall not be confined to development of generic skills but also focus on development of specific skills required by different groups of academic administrators in the system. The academic administrators have been categorized in different groups and key training needs have been identified. These needs have been mapped on to the training modules. Training methodologies and duration of training for meeting different kind of training needs have been spelt out. The guidelines provide for a centrally coordinated system for providing training and development opportunities through empanelled training providers. Since, this is likely to take some time, beginning shall be made to support proposals received from different academic, management and training institutions in the system. Certain special activities like support for training abroad, launching of diploma programme on planning and management in higher education, creating enabling environment for training of lower functional staff have also been included. With a view to manage the entire activity, a learning portal has been conceived.

In view of the multiplicity of activities and parameters, only broad financial parameters are provided in the guidelines. A National Committee which will steer and monitor the scheme, shall work out details of the activities on case to case basis. This would provide necessary flexibility in implementation of the scheme. Over a period of time, this would evolve into a full fledged system of meeting training and development needs of academic administrators in a variety of settings.

The guidelines have been put together on the basis of the deliberations made by the expert committee with inputs from different stake holders. The efforts made by the expert committee and other individuals/organizations are duly acknowledged.

Background

Higher education system in the country has expanded

rapidly over the last two decades. A large numbers of private institutions have also come up. Private institutions both aided by the government and the self financing institutions now outnumber government institutions. This has created intense competitive pressures. There are increased expectations of different stakeholders. Though the system still comprises predominantly of universities with large number of colleges affiliated to it, however, new forms of institutions have also significantly increased in numbers. These are deemed to be universities in many cases with multiple campuses, private universities, institutions of national importance set up by an Act of Parliament etc.

Higher education institutions not only cater to local body of students but are also seeking students from abroad. They are increasingly competing for talented students and competent faculty. They are expected to partner with industry and the research institutions in order to capitalize on their intellectual resources and also enhance employability of their graduates.

The changes above are putting pressures on administration of these institutions. The higher education institutions are no more insulated from the socio economic environment where they exist. They are expected to play a meaningful role in the socio economic development of the region. They are becoming key stakeholders in development of their respective regions.

Higher education institutions are presently managed either by teachers who have taken administrative responsibilities in addition or even to the exclusion of their primary responsibility for teaching and research or by people who have risen through ranks from the clerical cadre. This arrangement appears to be inadequate in the face of changing realities. There is an urgent need for adopting a professional approach towards administration of institutions of higher education in the country.

The National Policy on Higher Education 1986 and Programme of Action 1992 realized the importance of training and development of academic administrators. A committee was constituted for the purpose. The committee in its report on training and development of academic administrators recommended that a national level institution be set up for this. The report has been under consideration for some time. It is now felt that training and development of very large number of functionaries involved in administration of higher education institutions is not possible through a single national level institution. This objective can be better achieved by using the services of existing education and training institutions both within the university system and outside it, in a decentralized manner.

Introduction

These guidelines give a framework to ensure that academic administrators in the universities and colleges in the country to provide adequate opportunities for training and development in generic and specific areas of relevance to their work. The framework would seek to address the following key issues.

- Identification of groups of functionaries that should be covered and their training & development needs.
- Defining the framework for the implementation of the training & development programmes.
- Give broad guidelines for budgeting and funding.
- Map training needs to training modules and training programmes.
- Suggest pedagogy and instructional strategy for each kind of training.
- Provide guidelines for identifying, evaluating and empanelling hosts providers of training and

development programmes.

- Specify systems and processes for reviewing training programs so that periodically training programs can be Updated; Retired or Modified.
- Provide guidelines for systems and processes for overall coordination and management.

In the background above, these guidelines have been evolved for putting in place a structured system for providing training and development opportunities for academic administrators in the universities and colleges in the country.

Objective

The broad objective is to build capacity of the existing and prospective academic administrators to enable them to discharge their functions in a more professional manner. Through structured activities to be planned and taken up under this scheme, they will be made aware of the changing realties of their internal and external environment. Their competence shall be built by imparting them generic and specific skills and through their attitude transformation. These activities would create a sense of commitment and ensure that they work towards promoting excellence. Finally, this would help in creating a system of accountability through outcome focused monitoring. The thrust will be to achieve efficiency and effectiveness in planning and use of human, physical and financial facilities endowed with the institutions. This is to be achieved by ensuring delicate balance between the academic and managerial vision of the institution is maintained.

Academic Administrator

In guidelines, the term 'academic administrator' is used in a broad sense for all personnel concerned with the administration and management of universities. It includes teachers who are performing administrative functions (like hostel rectors and wardens, deans and directors of student welfare, international students' advisors etc.) and supervisors of campus activities (estate officer, security officer, university engineer and health officer).

To create four major groups of the various functionaries in the institutions of higher education to facilitate planning and implementation of training and development activities are as under.

5

Training and Development Its Role in Achieving Organisation

Is investment in the area of training and development linked to the bottom line within the business. Increasingly, high performing organisations today are recognising the need to use best training and development practices to enhance their competitive advantage. Training and development is an essential element of every business if the value and potential of it's people is to be harnessed and grown. Many studies have highlighted the clear links between well designed and strategic training and development initiatives and the bottom line within the business. The image of an industry and of individual employers is also influenced by the extent and quality of staff training and development. Potential employees in such an open labour market will assess the track record of prospective employers in this vital area. Career progression and development is an increasingly attractive or even basic requirement for many such employees. In today's business climate where all industries are experiencing staff and skills shortages, companies are faced with stiff internal and external competition for quality employees. Each employer who invests seriously in the area of Training and Development will reap the benefits of an enriched working environment with higher levels of staff retention as well as increased productivity and performance.

In a recent IBEC survey HR Benchmarking Report 2004, respondents were asked to identify the key drivers of training initiatives over the past year and for the 12 month period ahead. The top three were health and safety, technical changes and customer service. In other words, organisations are now using training and development as an incentive to retain and motivate their people and to be recognised as an employer of choice as well as giving staff the skills and knowledge needed to keep up with technological change and customer service. A further key finding in this survey was that the vast majority of companies surveyed (9 out of 10) stated they provided support to employees to pursue outside educational programmes. This support consisted of both financial aid as well as time off for both study and exam leave. Both of these initiatives may have benefits which are difficult to quantify, but areas such as staff turnover and morale are clear indicators of success in this field.

While research indicates an increased interest in and awareness of the benefits of training, the question needs to be asked as to whether this translated into Irish organisations establishing training policies and or increasing their spend on training. A National Survey of Training and Development in Ireland conducted by Garavan and Heraty in 2003 outlined a number of key trends which are emerging in the Training arena in Ireland. Some of the key ones include the following.

Irish organisations spend on average 3.55% of payroll on training which does not compare favourably with other EU member states. The IBEC HR Benchmarking Survey indicates a figure of 3.15%. The average number of days training provided per employee per year in 2004 was 5.35.

IBE CHR Benchmarking Survey indicates an average figure of 3 5 days. There is evidence of a positive attitude to training and development among those surveyed with many viewing it to be an important component in the organisation's strategy.

Smaller firms are more likely to deliver training in an ad hoc way with larger companies applying a more formal approach to managing training. Line managers and employees seem to have a greater role in the organisation and design of training and development. There is still a strong usage of the traditional forms of learning strategies including classroom teaching and subject driven courses, although there is a growth in the use of new technology to deliver training. Learning in teams is an increasingly popular form of learning in the workplace. Employees are now taking more personal ownership for their own development. However, the percentage spend and number of days spent training staff may be useful in order to get an overview of the companies commitment to training and development, but it is the manner, approach and content of the training initiatives as well as their assessment and follow up which determine success. It is all too easy to throw money at a performance problem and assume that a training course will sort it out, when this may well be just putting a plaster over an open wound.

Training initiatives need to be strategically aligned to the overall company mission and goals. They need to be designed and delivered with the aim of helping staff to achieve their departmental as well as personal goals, so the trend of increased involvement by line managers and employees is a positive development in terms of ownership of the training and learning. By adopting a strategic approach to training and development rather than an unplanned and ad hoc one, training and development initiatives become more targeted, measurable and effective.

However, increased flexibility in terms of training delivery may need to be expanded in the future to facilitate participant's different learning styles as well as lifestyles. They also need to be assessed in terms of reaction, learning, behaviour change and results to determine the added value to the organisation.

This area of evaluation is one whereby many organisations simply evaluate the effectiveness of the training intervention based on the initial reaction of participants, an area which clearly needs to be expanded. A sample training and development approach is outlined below describing the essential elements in a strategic approach.

Development of Training and Development Plan

Types of training and development required Knowledge Skills Attitudinal Personal Development Continuing Professional Development (CPD) Establishment of standardsGap in current knowledge, skills, attitude levels

Selection of Training Methods

On the job methods "Sitting by Nelly, Coaching, Mentoring, In house courses Off the job methods Work placement, External courses, Distance learning, Workshops Design of in house programmes Participation in externally run programmes

Implementing Training and Development

Selection of participants
Staff scheduling
Recording of training undertaken
Conducting and or facilitating training and development

Evaluating Training and Development Process

Measurement of results against standards
Reaction Learning Behaviour Results

In order to remain competitive and to ensure excellent staff are attracted to and remain within the organisation, companies need to ensure that the training and development of all employees is an issue which is taken seriously. By investing in the development of the people who are the face of the business, companies can get ahead of the competition and excel in what they do. One of the most important aspects of managing people lies in helping employees become more effective at their jobs and being able to adapt to that job or another job as heshe matures within the organisation. This requires a high level of co ordination between employee training and development and the range of other personnel functions, such as recruitment and selection, performance appraisal, reward systems and employee relations.

Identification of a company's training needs, designing a relevant training plan, selecting and implementing the resulting training programme and evaluating it's success are therefore integral elements of the overall Human Resource process. However, for any of these functions to be effective, the Training plans and policies must be in line with the organisation's strategic objectives. The Training function is increasingly considered to be a key player in helping the organisation to achieve it's goals through it's people as it is becoming more generally accepted that there is a strong correlation between organisational success and investment in training and development. There is now a growing awareness of the importance of a planned approach to training and development as a tool for competitive advantage, staff recruitment, selection, retention and motivation.

The whole Training and Development function has increasingly acquired status as the instrument for breaking new ground and bringing about change through its developmental activities. Training managers must provide expert advice to top level management, usually about the value to the organisation of a particular kind of training. Furthermore, they must have the means to persuade management as to a systematic approach to training outlining for example, the extent to which changes in structure and procedures will be necessary to support training. The training must take place within a framework of partnership between the trainer, employer and employee.

This relationship must be characterised by trust between all stakeholders so that training does not simply reflect the views of the employer. This commonality of interest must be identified and worked towards. Training and development is about making a difference to the bottom line, both in terms of how people feel about their jobs as well as in the area of performance and productivity. Ultimately, it is about adding real value to the organisation and those who comprise it.

Personnel Training And Development

Policy It is the policy of the State of North Carolina to provide training and development for its employees designed to.

- Improve productivity, effectiveness and efficiency of government service by development and better utilization of talents, abilities and potential of employees.
- Help employees develop their knowledge, skills and abilities so that they might become better qualified to perform the duties of their present jobs and advance to more responsible positions.
- Provide for the development of managers and supervisors capable of organizing and developing effective management systems for the accomplishment of each State agency's goals and objectives.

- Accelerate the development of culturally disadvantaged employees whose abilities and aptitudes are underutilized because of inadequate education and training.

- Alleviate labor market shortages and reduce personnel turnover.

- Prepare employees to deal more effectively with growing social, scientific and economic problems faced by government by making use of advances in professional and vocational knowledge and technology.

Responsibility Providing adequate training and development of State employees can best be accomplished through the combined efforts of employees, supervisors on the job, departmental management and the Office of State Personnel in cooperation with the State's institutions of higher education. Training and development programs should recognize the following roles. Employees. State employees at all levels ultimately retain an obligation for their own development and education and it is expected that employees will advance their own careers through appropriate self education and selfimprovement.

Managers and Supervisors. Managers and supervisors have the initial responsibility for training and development of their employees. In fulfilling this responsibility, managers and supervisors should identify the individual training needs of their employees, and work with employees to prepare and effect plans for their development. Such plans should make use of on the job training including individual and group instruction by supervisors, formal training and educational activities, and rotational assignments to provide greater depth and a wide base of experience.

Agencies. Each agency has a responsibility for training and developing its employees. It is responsible for assuring that training programs geared to specific agency needs are planned, budgeted and established and that their employees participate in these programs. In addition each agency shall work closely with other agencies and the Office of State Personnel to promote the use of interagency training programs and resources wherever possible.

Office of State Personnel. The Office of State Personnel shall be responsible for the State's role in overall planning, coordinating and review of training and development programs and appropriate interagency training.

State Universities, the Community College System and Public

Instruction. The Office of State Personnel and State agencies are responsible for utilizing the State's universities, community college system, and public instruction to the fullest degree possible in securing professional, management and vocational education to meet their personnel development needs.

Use of Non State Government Education and Training

Sources Policy. State agencies may enter into contracts for education and training through non State government sources in accordance with established State Personnel Commission policies and procedures. All contracts should follow policies and procedures issued by the Division of Purchase and Contract, Department of Administration.

Determination of Need for Training

Before State Personnel authorizes education or training through non State government sources, the agency must have.

- Determined that agency employees do not possess the knowledge and skills to meet that training or educational need, and

- Determined that training is not available within State government to meet the agency's needs. Education and training are not available when.

* Existing programs in State government will not meet the need

* New programs cannot be established to meet need

* Inquiry has failed to disclose availability of programs in other departments, State Personnel, public education, higher education institutions or elsewhere in State government.

Selection of Non Government Sources

When there is a choice between outside training sources, consideration will be given to the following factors.

- Competency to provide the particular training needed
- Geographic accessibility of the training source
- Availability of training at the particular time or place it is needed
- Comparative cost as determined by Division of Purchase and Contract policies and procedures
- Practicality of administrative arrangement involved
- The significance of accreditation
- The advantages that might result from arrangements with the source when several equally acceptable are available
- The consequences of using limited State resources versus none at all

Procedure for Approval of Non State Sources

Should any State agency have an educational or training

need that cannot be met by resources within State government, the following steps must be followed.

1. The agency's training needs and training objectives must be defined. This should include an explanation of how the achievement of these training objectives contribute to the agency's goals.

2. Upon agreement by the Office of State Personnel that such training cannot be obtained within State government resources, the Division of Purchase and Contract should be notified of the training need through the submission of a justification memo 1 North Carolina Administrative Code 5C. This request should be coordinated through the agency's purchasing officer.

3. It must be documented in the justification memo that the educational or training need cannot reasonably be met by any State government institution or agency. This should include a list of the agencies contacted and the responses of each agency.

4. The required training will then be acquired in accordance with State Purchase and Contract Policy.

Apprenticeship Training

It is policy of the State of North Carolina to promote and encourage the establishment, maintenance and growth of apprenticeship programs to help meet the workforce needs of State government. All such program shall be administered through and in accordance with policy and standards established by the North Carolina Department of Labor in cooperation with the employing agency. All persons serving in an apprenticeship program supported by funding from a permanent position subject to the State

Personnel Act shall receive a regular trainee appoinment. An apprenticeship trainee appointment to a permanent position may be preceded by a time limited appointment to an apprenticeship slot. An apprentice with a trainee or time limited appointment shall receive the same employment benefits as other SPA employees with trainee or time limited appointments. Upon successful completion of an apprenticeship program, an apprentice who enters regular state employment shall receive a permanent appointment.

6

Ethics Training and Development in the Military

In June 2006, the Pentagon announced that all US servicemen in Iraq were to undergo additional military ethics training, including lessons in "core warrior values." Lieutenant General Peter Chiarelli, then commander of the Multinational Corps in Iraq, said that the training would focus on "professional military values and the importance of disciplined, professional conduct in combat." This highlighted the growing importance of ethics training and development in themilitary, not just for the forces of theUnited States but for those of other countries as well. Formal ethics training programs were a rarity inmost armed forces until fairly recently. In the past decade, they have become increasingly common. The Canadian Department of National Defence, for instance, introduced a "Defence Ethics Program" in 1997, and the French military academy at St. Cyr began its program in ethics training in 2002.

It is one thing to say that soldiers will have to undergo ethics training, it is quite another to ensure that they learn the right lessons. Indeed, if incorrectly carried out, ethics training might even be counterproductive. It is clear from a survey of ethics training programs in various national militaries that there is no uniformity of approach between themand a lack of coherence within them. There is also disagreement as to the degree to which such programs are necessary in the first place.Given the fact that fewWestern nations now send their military forces on operations independently, the lack of uniformity about what constitutes ethical behavior and how best to educate soldiers is potentially a cause for alarm. As Major General Patrick Cordingley, former commander of the 7th Armoured Brigade in the British Army, noted after a recent trip to Afghanistan, although rules of engagement for the various coalition forces in that country are similar, they are interpreted in different ways. We need, he said, to get together as a coalition and thrash out the ethics behind the rules in order to reach mutual understanding.

It is obvious that much needs to be done in determining what is the best approach to instilling the desired ethics in servicemen and women. This article builds on a workshop on "Ethics Training and Development in the Military," held at the University ofHull in the UnitedKingdomon 22 23 June 2006. Thisworkshopwas attended by representatives fromthe armed forces and military academies of ten countries, as well as philosophers, political scientists, and historians. Theworkshop sought to determinewhat ethics training and development programs are in existence; their theoretical underpinnings, the effect of cultural and national differences on content; whether such programs are best run by military officers, chaplains, lawyers, or academic philosophers, and if it is feasible to develop common principles and approaches for the armed forces of participating countries. The article summarizes and expands on the initial directions identified by participants, and aims thereby to provide greater understanding of amatter requiring further thought, amatter that is becoming a vital force influencing the battlefields of the twenty first century.

The Importance of Ethics Training and Development

The first issues to be resolved are why ethics matter to the military and whether formal ethics training programs are actually necessary or productive. These issues raise the question ofwhat wemean bymilitary "ethics." Are we referring to the instillation inmilitary personnel of a general morality that makes them what an ordinary civilian might consider "morally good". Or are we referring more narrowly to the professional standard required for the fulfilment of their role as servicemen and women. Is it actually necessary formilitary personnel to bemorally good as long as they are proficient at their jobs. Are the two separable, or are they mutually dependent. In short, are the ethics required of a soldier in his or her role role morality) the same as those required of a civilian.

Paul Robinson is an Associate Professor in Public and International Affairs at the University of Ottawa, Canada, and until recently was a lecturer in security studies, and deputy director of the Institute of Applied Ethics, at the University of Hull, England. He has also served as an officer in the British and Canadian armies. Dr. Robinson is the author of numerous works onmilitary history, defense policy, andmilitary ethics, including most recently the book Military Honour and the Conduct of War. FromAncientGreece to Iraq.

In a paper about the system of ethics training at the US Military Academy atWest Point, Lieutenant Colonel JeffreyWilson notes the opinion expressed by the late General Maxwell Taylor, who saw no moral problems in serving with a combat ready officer who is 'loyal to his superiors and his profession but disloyal to his wife, or keeps physically fit but has 'General Grant'sweakness for strong drink.'For Taylor, a good soldier, even a good officer, could be a bad man. It is instructive to examine this question from the point of view of the combat soldier.When under fire, does he worry whether the man next to him is an adulterer, or merely whether he is brave and knows how to use hisweapon.Almost certainly the latter. Indeed, one can findmany examples of outstanding military officers whose personal lives left much to be desired. For example, General Sir Arthur Currie, commander of the Canadian Corps in the latter half of the First World War, embezzled regimental funds while a battalion commander.

But he was to prove himself one of the best generals serving on the Western Front. As Lieutenant ColonelWilson also points out, General Taylor's position eventually became unsustainable due to a succession of scandals which undermined public faith in the military in the years following the Second World War. The armed forces of the world are under increasing public scrutiny, and if their members behave in a fashionwhich the public deemsmorally reprehensible it may destroy public support for their mission. We live in the era of the strategic corporal. Immoral behavior by even the lowest ranking soldier can have a strategic effect, aswitnessed by the impact of the images of PrivateLynndie England, a strategic private, atAbuGhraib prison in Iraq. When viewed in this manner, the conflict between role and ordinary morality is overcome, as thatwhich is contrary to ordinarymorality indirectly undermines the mission by destroying public support, and is therefore also contrary to role morality. As Hilliard Aronovitch concluded in a 2001 article in Journal of Applied Philosophy. Effective fighters are also ethical fighters good soldiers in the one sense are also good soldiers in the other sense. Hence, good soldiers must in certain ways be good persons as well.

Given this conclusion, it would appear that it is highly desirable to institute some form of ethical development for service men and women. That does not necessarilymean, however, that formal ethics training is the answer. The traditional way of approaching this matter has been to use a form of osmosis, in which military institutions shaped the characters of their members by unseen and gradual influences. The sheer force of the institutions, via their historical traditions, their atmosphere, and the example and pressure of the soldiers' peers, would mold the character of the trainee into the desired form without any official ethics training. This is indeed still themethod relied on to a large degree by the British armed forces, who conduct very little in the way of formal ethics training. In their defense, the British would undoubtedly claimthat their methodology works. There is no evidence that British service men andwomen behave worse than soldiers of other countries withmore formal systems. However,many would stipulate that the ability ofmilitary institutions to indirectly influence the character of their members has declined. Once all soldiers weremale; they joined at a young age; lived together in barracks; few married, and when they did it was after years of service. Participation and regular attendance at the corporals', sergeants', or officers' mess was more or less compulsory; one could not escape the powerful influence of the institution. Today, however, troops often join the force later in life, when their characters are fairly developed. They marry earlier and are more likely to live off post; military messes and clubs are in decline. One cannot rely on the social system to integrate new members of the force through some hidden process of osmosis.

This lack of social influences makes a formal systemof ethics training desirable. There are, however, some dangers. If we teach people that they must be "moral" and that their institution demands and upholds the highest standards, there is always a danger that members of those institutions will come to regard themselves as morally superior to those outside the military. Perversely, anything they do then becomes moral in their eyes, because they are "good" and so whatever they do must be good.

In short, one can argue that thismeans ethics educationmust avoid the spirit of elitism. Acommon refrain among military officers is that moral standards in society are in decline and the military has the responsibility of being morally superior to the general public. According to Andrew Bacevich's book The New American Militarism. "In a 2003 survey of American] military personnel, 'two thirds [of those polled said they think military members have higher moral standards than the nation they serve. Once in the military, many said, members are wrapped in a culture that values honor and morality.

Admiral Stanley Arthur, US Navy Retired, has expressed concern that 'more andmore, enlisted as well as officers are beginning to feel that they are special, better than the society they serve. This viewis potentially dangerous, a point made by a former commander of the German Zentrum für Innere Führung Leadership Development and Civic Education Center, who argued that the aim of ethics educationmust be to ensure that the ethics of soldiers coincide as closely as possible with the society they serve, ensuring that soldiers continue to view themselves as citizens, not asmembers of some special caste.According to StefanWerdelis, theGerman approach is to viewthe "soldier as citizen in uniform. Given their historical experience of military elites, the Germans' distrust of themis understandable. Other countries, which have hadmore positive experiences, might be justified in feeling less concern. It is clear, however, that there is disagreement about what the end result of ethics training in the military should be.

Who Owns Ethics Training in the Military

If one accepts the hypothesis that some form of ethics training is desirable, the next question iswho should be responsible for it. There are a number of possible candidates. military officers, lawyers, chaplains, and civilian philosophers being the obvious choices. Different countries utilize each of these professions in different ways, resulting in considerable disagreement about who should "own" ethics training.

Amajor difference is between the "top down" and "bottom up" approaches to ethics in the military. The Canadian Defence Ethics Program and the German systemof Innere Führung are examples of centrally directed programs which operate across all services according to a common, centrally dictated, set of principles. This methodology has considerable advantages. Above all, it ensures coherence. The danger with the top down approach is that ethics training often comes to be viewed as yet another chore imposed on junior commanders from on high, as a check the box requirement. Giving the leading role in ethics training to those at lower levels of the chain of command, and allowing for differences between units and services is one way of overcoming such perceptions. The two approaches may not, however, be incompatible; ideally, units may have a centrally operated program that outlines the principles and provides training for the trainers, while the actual management is conducted at the lower levels of the organization.

In the United States, according to Dr. Martin Cook of the United States Air Force Academy, the systemof ethics training suffers fromincoherence. Numerous activities exist side by side, each introduced in response to some previous ethics initiative or scandal, with little or no effort at integration. What one sees, says Dr. Cook, is a fundamentally incoherent and confused welter of programs justified, if at all, by the belief that if ethics is important, throwing lots of resources at the subject from any number of angles and approaches must somehow be doing some good. One obvious area of disagreement concerns the role of chaplains in ethics training. According to Colonel Yvon Desjardins, director of the Canadian Defence Ethics Program, the Canadian Forces deliberately keep military chaplains away from ethics training. By contrast, chaplains play a major role in the German Zentrumfür Innere Führung, and the ethics program of the Norwegian military is entirely dominated by the chaplains' corps. Chaplains in the Norwegianmilitary play a key role in creating the list of core military values, conductingmuch of the actual training, and are extremely active in the research and publishing associated withmilitary ethics. The difference in approach may in part be explained by differing national characteristics. Bearing in mind Canada's multicultural nature, and the fact that Canadian military members are of diverse religious backgrounds often choosing not to exercise strong religious beliefs), the CF believe that their members might not react positively to what might be viewed as religious indoctrination. This is especially true if training is conducted by chaplains of a different religious affiliation.Norway, however, is a religiously homogenous nation, being 85 percent Lutheran.Aprogramdominated by Lutheran pastors is unlikely under such circumstances to meet resistance. Having said that, Norwegian chaplains involved in ethics training insist that their model could be applied elsewhere, noting that there is no reason why a secular humanist should have any more authority with, say, Muslim soldiers than would a Christian chaplain. Quite the contrary, they claim, noting that chaplains in many armed forces often already cater to the pastoral needs of members of other religious affiliations. It is safe to say that there is no final agreement as to what the appropriate role of chaplains should be in ethics training.

Furthermore, the influence of chaplains may sometimes be less than that of religious institutions and personalities outside the military, and the influence of the latter is not always beneficial. Allegations in 2005 of "religious pressure" being exerted on cadets at theUSAir ForceAcademy bearwitness to this dilemma.Dr. Cook comments that "the kinds of independent and nondenominational Evangelical churchesmany cadets choose to attend Colorado Springs being an 'Evangelical Vatican' serve to instill a resistance to critical thinking and complexity in ethical reflection they inculcate a kind of anti intellectualism when it comes to ethical reflection that is often quite difficult to penetrate in the classroom. The role of religion and religious authorities in military education appears to require further investigation.

There is also debate as to the role that philosophers might play in military ethics education. It is generally felt that it is pointless to attempt to instill the rank and file with formal lessons in moral philosophy. Lectures on deontology, utilitarianism, or other philosophical systems often are not seen as directly relevant to the practical needs of the soldier. There are indeed pitfalls in entirely excluding philosophers fromwhat is after all their intellectual terrain. Patrick Mileham of the British Centre for Defense and International Security Studies has drawn attention to this conundrumin a discussion of ethics training in the British armed forces. British units have, Mileham claims, remained resistant to the idea of properly researching the subject of moral philosophy, in order to apply its findings to doctrine, teaching, and publications.

What they have produced by way of doctrine muddles what Mileham terms institutional ethics" domestic regulation in barracks and human re sourcemanagement with operational ethics" howsoldiers ought to behave on active duty or in combat).This hostility to philosophy had a negative effect, some claim, in the production of the British Army's ethics doctrine, as outlined in the pamphlet Values and Standards of the British Army, published in 2000. The pamphlet follows a virtue ethics approach, detailing the virtues required of the soldier, and implying that the way to ensure proper ethical behavior is through the inculcation of the necessary virtues. However, the pamphlet goes on to contradict its previous emphasis on virtue by stating that when determining what to do, soldiers should follow a utilitarian Service Test. Have the actions or behavior of an individual adversely impacted or are they likely to impact on the efficiency or operational effectiveness of the Army."

The mixing of virtue ethics and utilitarianismin this fashion is intellectually incoherent and confusing to the novice. Consultation with a moral philosopher could have avoided this contradiction. Dr. Mileham reports, however, that there is now near critical mass of serving officers in all three services calling for a joint services approach and reflecting the need for professional, independent study of moral conduct, doctrine, publications, and training. The British Army's doctrine manual Land Operations, published in 2005, contains a chapter on The Moral Component and presents a much better explanation of the "Values and Standards required of individuals.Although some leaders may not want philosophers lecturing the rank and file, it is nonetheless desirable for those charged with the responsibility for teaching military ethics to have some philosophical training. If, for instance, ethics instructors are using case studies as a teaching method, they can only do so effectively if they have some knowledge of the concepts the case studies aremeant to demonstrate.One can well argue that there is a legitimate need for some philosophy education for allmilitary officers. In fact, Dr. Cook notes that cadets at the US Air Force Academy generally consider their required philosophy course "one of the very best in the core curriculum. Often they comment that its relevance to their future careers is quite obvious."

On What Principles Should Ethics Training be Based

Even though there is an acrimonious debate over who should "own" ethics training in the military, there is greater consensus regarding the principles on which such training should be based, although there are some dissenting voices. The first area of disagreement concerns the goal to which ethics training is directed. The most commonly expressed sentiment among those taskedwith the conduct of this training is that the objective should be individuals who are able to think about ethical problems independently and act "autonomously." Individuals should understand thatwhat they believe is right ismore important than merely obeying orders or succumbing to peer pressure.

Lawrence Kohlberg developed a famous though disputed model ofmoral development which includes three levels. the pre conventional level, in which individuals act correctly primarily in order to avoid punishment; a conventional level, where they respond to peer pressure, and are driven by a concern for reputation; and a post conventional level duringwhich individuals use their own reasoning to determine "universal ethical principles" of right and wrong, and then abide by them because they have "seen the validity of principles and become committed to them." Most practitioners feel that the aim of ethics training should be tomove soldiers up the ladder toward the post conventional stage. The objective should be to train soldiers who act ethically, not because they've been told to, or because they think it willmake themlook good, but because they themselves have determined that it is the right thing to do. Otherwise, they may acquiesce to unethical orders or peer pressure.

There are those who believe that this inculcation is too ambitious a goal. Peter Olsthoorn of the Royal Netherlands Military Academy notes that concern for reputation (level two of Kohlberg's model) plays a vital part in military life the desire not to look bad in front of one's colleagues is amajor reason why soldiers show courage in battle. Drawing on Mark Osiel's book ObeyingOrders,Olsthoorn argues that in amilitary environment, "we should be somewhat less stringent accepting that moral rules are followed, not because they aremoral, but because not following thembrings disesteem. Whatever the desired end state, the approach adopted in most armed forces is that of virtue ethics, with their philosophical origins found in Aristotle. Essentially, virtue ethics seeks to ensuremoral behavior by instilling certain virtues (loyalty, honesty, and courage) to create good character. The person with character will then behave appropriately because that is the sort of person he or she is. The advantage, from a military point of view, of this approach is that in combat there are intense pressures and little time for deep intellectual philosophizing. In such situations having an individual who will behave properly due to conditioned responses is highly desirable. Consequently,manymilitary academies have adopted an approach based on Aristotelian virtue ethics. Those in the United States are prime examples. Quoting Lieutenant Colonel Wilson, "The US Military Academy takes great pains to instill essentially Aristotelian virtues into the cadets in order to build a character worthy of trust." Dr. Cook comments that at theUSAir ForceAcademy, "It's rather obvious that Aristotle is the intellectual father of the enterprise."

Regardless of their genesis, most armed forces have produced lists of the virtues they claimto value. These vary fromcountry to country and service to service, but have considerable overlap. The United States Army lists its "Army Values" as.

- Loyalty
- Duty
- Respect
- Selfless Service
- Honor
- Integrity
- Personal Courage

By contrast, the "Core Values" of the British Army are.

- Selfless Commitment
- Courage

- Discipline
- Integrity
- Loyalty
- Respect for Others

While those of the Canadian Forces are.

- Duty
- Loyalty
- Integrity
- Courage

The similarities between lists suggests that there is a common core ofmilitary virtues on which a universal moral code might be constructed. There are, however, criticisms of the virtue ethics approach. In particular, the emphasis on character might have the effect of causing military leaders to believe that all unethical behavior is the product of failures of character ("few bad apples" theory). Many times such failures are the product of deficiencies in institutions or practices. The focus on character may prevent leaders from taking a critical look at the institutions they lead and thereby ensure that morally corrupting rules, structures, and systems remain. Teaching soldiers that theymust be brave, loyal, and so forth, does not tell themwhat to do when there are conflicts between the requirements of various virtues. Virtue ethics needs to go beyond mere rote learning of lists of virtues in an attempt to teach soldiers to reason and understand exactly what the virtues mean and howto resolve conflicts between them.Unfortunately, this is not always the case in teaching military ethics.

Another criticism of the virtue ethics approach comes from Professor Asa Kasher, author of the Code of Ethics of the Israel Defense Forces (IDF). He argues that since the focus of mostWestern armed forces, as well as the justification of most wars, in recent years, has been humanitarian intervention and peacekeeping operations, it makes little sense to teach soldiers only "military" ethics.Kasher advocates an appropriate combination of military and police ethics. The latter, he maintains, requires a different set of virtues.

Similarly a number of British ethicists dislike the use of the term "warrior," which in the eyes of at least some is associated not with noble soldiers but savages with spears. This distinction is also made by the American author Ralph Peters who distinguishes between soldiers and warriors. Warriors are "erratic primitives of shifting allegiance, habituated to violence, with no stake in civil order. Unlike soldiers, warriors do not play by our rules, do not respect them, and do not obey orders they do not like." Warrior ethics and virtues according to such interpretations are undesirable, especially in an age where soldiers are rarely involved in direct combat, but aremore likely to conduct "operations other than war." These operations require a very different approach to that of the traditional combat soldier. Others, on the other hand, point out that combat remains the fundamental task for armed forces, and its requirement should continue to underpin professional ethics.

Professor Kasher also comments that military ethics should not be ethics applied to the broad category ofmilitary affairs, but rather a concept directly related to what constitutes correct behavior for military personnel. He believes the objective "is not to build appropriate character, but rather appropriate behavior. Kasher complains thatmany of the lists of virtues and values contain the same virtues and values that anybody outside the military might agree with. This, he feels, is the wrong approach. In the IDF, ethics training begins with the development of professional identity, not with conventional morality. Soldiers in modern democracies tend to be moral relativists.

They regard talk of morality as an external imposition. But if you talk in terms of professional development and identity they are more accepting. Instead of starting with lists of virtues and attempting to indoctrinate the individual soldier, one needs to first expose the individual to what it means to be a soldier in a democratic state. This means that the starting point of ethics training should be the principles of liberal democracy, its values and norms.

Such a methodology leads one away from a "virtue" approach and more toward a "values based" one (virtues representing desirable characteristics of individuals, such as courage; and values representing the ideals that the community cherishes, such as freedom . There are ethics training programs such as that of the Canadian Department of National Defence that are in part values based the program is a hybrid of values based and compliance based elements). However, the lists of values produced in these programs are often similar to the lists of virtues required of any ideal military person, and the distinction between values and virtues is not always clear.

What Should Ethics Training Courses Contain.

A vital issue is the content of ethics training courses. As previously noted, training in moral philosophy may be desirable for leaders, though not necessarily for more junior personnel. There is, however, universal agreement that to be effective, ethics training should be practically oriented and relevant to the soldier, sailor, or airman. Addressing instances of immoral behavior by simply giving another lecture on "warrior values" is unlikely to generate much of an effect.

In dealing with instances of immoral behavior most practitioners favor the use of case studies. Unfortunately, there are few suitable case studies readily available. In the English language the majority of the studies are American.

The increased production of suchmaterials for use by instructors would certainly be welcomed. Motivational speakers are also popular at many institutions, but a number of ethics instructors have expressed doubt regarding their utility. Pep talks to soldiers by successful coaches, businesspeople, or even beauty queens, do not necessarily touch soldiers'hearts. Such "experts" are often viewed as being too remote from the soldier's practical experience. Most institutions and services have found it is best to use motivational speakers with military experience and knowledge. Similarly, if role models are depicted in books, ormuseumdisplays, considerable care needs to be given to ensuring that the model presented is appropriate to the soldier's frame of reference.

At the recent workshop held at Hull University in England, several useful points were made regarding the use of case studies. Anumber of workshop participants thought it productive to start with simpler cases and move onto more complex ones. One approach is to get soldiers to generate case studies of their own, based on personal experiences. The individual soldiers can talk to their colleagues about the case, what happened, and whether they think that the right thing was done. Alternatively, cases can be chosen to illustrate moral dilemmas, which soldiers then have to resolve. This encourages people to think about various solutions, rather than simply being told the "right" answer.

Unfortunately, there is an almost universal tendency to use negative cases when illustrating ethical or unethical behavior. This is often the case even when soldiers present their own cases they nearly always pick a case in which an individual has misbehaved, and the discussion then centers around what was bad about the behavior and why things went wrong. While negative cases can make a contribution, it would be more useful to the inculcation of appropriate responses if more positive examples were used. The focus on negative cases may indirectly instill the idea that the point of ethics training is to teach personnel to avoid making mistakes, rather than training them to act in an exemplary manner. The use of negative ethical examples relates to another problem, the fact that ethics trainingwhen not properly conductedmay create a climate advocating risk avoidance. Ethics may be viewed as something one resorts to only after a scandal, as a form of cover up. Certainly, the manner in which ethics programs have evolved in various countries indicates this is often the case. Martin Cook notes this tendency in the US armed forces. He believes it may explain the incoherence of American ethics training after a particular scandal a new training course or ethics institution is set up. These actions are to serve as an indication that something is being done to rectify the problem however, the real problem lies in the fact that no action is taken to integrate these new courses or institutions with existing ones.

The lesson one may draw from this is that ethics training should not be seen as some supplement which one puts on top of other forms of military training late in the daywhen there happens to be a sparemoment in the timetable. Ethics training needs to be seen as something other than a burdensome compulsory duty. Rather it needs to be integrated intomilitary training froma very early stage as a fundamental part of the process of developing professional soldiers. This alsomeans that ethics courseswhich formpart of the curriculum at military academies might in some cases be usefully moved forward to appear earlier than they currently do. It also means that ethics needs to be integrated intomilitary exercises and pre deployment training for operations, so that it becomes a part of regular military life.

Conclusion

According to General Cordingley, "Our soldiers are not

little angels. We need to be realistic. Ethics training by itself will not produce morally perfect soldiers. A few extra lectures on warrior values are unlikely to transform the behavior of soldiers in Iraq and elsewhere. Aneed still exists for the informal processes of institutional and peer pressure designed to help shape and develop character, which also means leaders must continually examine the health of their institutions. There is little point in teaching individuals a particular formof behavior, if they can see that the institution to which they belong in practice rewards and values other behavior.

Moral leadership is, therefore, a vital supplement to formal ethics training. It is vital that leaders foster a culture which encourages ethical debate. Jamie Cullens, director of the Center for Defence Leadership Studies at the Australian Defense College, has pointed out that the Australian Defense Force has sought to create an organizational culture which is willing to discuss past errors as well as to promote traditions emphasizing military achievements and positive examples of military ethics and national values. Through programs of this sort, one can hope to tackle ethical issues before, not after, the next disaster.To conclude, some form of formal training appears to be desirable. Additionally, there is a need to establish a common set of values that might be used in coalition warfare. It is also clear that there is little agreement among Western democratic nations as to how we might institute this training.

This lack of consensus may be unavoidable. Differences in national character and historymaymake themodels of one country unsuitable for another. Nevertheless, we need to learn from one another. It is hoped that the thoughts, programs, and methodologies presented in this article might enlighten those charged with the weighty responsibility of ethics training in the military.

7

Training and Development

Identification of Training and Development Needs

Managers are expected to discuss training and development needs with each of their staff at least annually as part of the Performance Review and Planning process. The training and development needs of staff newly appointed to their positions should be discussed within four weeks of their taking up the position, whether or not they are new to the University.

Staff of the Training and Development Unit are available to assist managers or individual staff to identify training needs and can advise on appropriate ways to meet identified needs. These include mentoring, coaching, attendance at an internal or external course, or completion of a qualification. Any staff member may contact TDU staff directly for confidential advice, and assistance can be provided on a one to one basis.

Internal Training and Development Sessions

The Training and Development Unit organises training for staff on all campuses sites and can set up specific sessions to meet identified needs for a department or section, group of departments, or occupational group. Computing Services also administers an on going programme of courses for staff and other University sections and departments offer training sessions for staff as needs arise.

Enrolment

All new staff are expected to enrol with the TDU for the University induction programme as soon as practicable after they take up their duties, and, if teaching staff, for the Teaching Skills Development Programme. New staff who have a teaching qualification or who have held a university teaching position for at least three years may, if they wish, apply in writing through their HOD (or equivalent) to the Director of Training and Development for consideration for a full or partial exemption from the Teaching Skills Development Programme. Enrolments for training provided by other sections or departments should be made direct to the provider.

Costs

Costs of courses organised by the Training and Development Unit are met by the centralised training and development budget administered by the TDU. Additional courses may on occasion be arranged on a cost recovery basis. Where staff enrolled on any TDU course withdraw within 48 hours of the beginning of the course (or do not attend), a charge may be levied on departments or sections to meet per capita expenses incurred. Any charging arrangements for sessions not offered through the TDU are made by the provider. Budget centre managers may contract external trainers to conduct training for their staff, using funds from either the Training and Development allocation of their PIA budget (where the training is predominantly for staff paid for the PIA budget) or from appropriate non PIA sources under their control.

If it is intended to invite other staff from within their College or Division and to expect them to contribute to the cost, arrangements should be made through the budget centre managers of those staff or through the relevant Pro or Assistant Vice Chancellor's Office. Managers are encouraged to consult with the Director TDU when planning such training and are required to do so where the training involves staff from more than one College or Division. In all cases managers are asked to check that they do not set dates that clash with other training planned for the same target group.

Enrolment for University Courses

In the interests of staff development, staff are encouraged to enrol for Massey University courses relevant to their employment in accordance with the applicable employment contract provided the amount of study being undertaken will not impinge upon their ability to carry out their paid duties. All staff will be required to comply with the enrolment regulations relating to registration, course approval and withdrawal from papers.

A manager may meet, from their own budget, some or all of the tuition costs to enable a staff member to obtain relevant qualifications, other than a doctorate, from another tertiary institution if the qualification is not obtainable at Massey University, or where it was agreed at the time of appointment that the staff member could complete a programme of study already commenced at another institution. The granting of such tuition costs each year shall be subject to the staff member making satisfactory progress in their work and studies.

Academic Staff

Staff contemplating enrolling for PhDs at other universities are required to submit their programme through their Head of Department (or equivalent) to the Doctoral Research Committee. Newly appointed academic staff from outside the University who are already part way through a doctoral programme relevant to their new position at another university may be granted approval to continue by the appropriate Pro Vice Chancellor, when it is not practicable for them to transfer their registration to Massey. Budget centre managers may agree to meet some of all of the fees for approved study at other universities from their own budget provided that such fees are not a charge against a PIA budget unless the staff member is paid from that budget.

General Staff

Approval is not normally given for general staff to enrol for a PhD. Consideration will, however, be given to applications from general staff who meet academic entry requirements and have the support of their Head of Department, subject to the following conditions.

> the applicant holds no more than 80% of a full time appointment;
>
> the University is not meeting the fees; and
>
> it is clearly understood that attainment of a PhD does not imply any undertaking or obligation on the part of the University to transfer the applicant to an academic appointment.

Fees Waiver for Massey University Courses

The following provisions apply to staff employed under the main Massey employment contract. Exemption of fees may be granted to eligible staff who are New Zealand citizens or permanent residents or Australian citizens or otherwise eligible for domestic fees. All staff other than casuals are entitled to have the normal enrolment fee, students' association and student counselling fees waived. Casual staff are not eligible for a fees waiver. Tuition fee concessions apply to part time staff on a pro rata basis. Staff are not exempt from the late enrolment fee or tuition fees payable after any fee concession, granted or declined, has been applied to their programme of study. Staff who leave the employment of the University before the end of a semester may be required to pay the fees for that semester.

Any financial support for block courses, or for any full fee courses such as the Master of Business Administration (MBA) degree, is normally limited to the cost of tuition for an equivalent amount of permissible internal study, inclusive of any internal or extramural papers being taken at the same time.

Academic Staff

Academic staff employed on a contract of at least three years' duration and whose salaries are paid though bulk funding revenue, and all graduate assistants, may have Massey University tuition fees paid centrally for approved internal and extramural study relevant to their appointment. Academic staff whose salaries are paid by full cost recovery centres or through research or other externally funded contracts in departments and who are employed on a contract of at least three years' duration may have tuition fees for approved internal or extramural study paid by their budget centre manager. Budget centre managers may choose to pay fees for staff on shorter contracts. Tutors and senior tutors will not have fees waived for PhD study. Staff employed on a contract of at least three years' duration may apply for a fees exemption for up to 35 points of approved internal or extramural study in any one year. Budget centre managers may apply for permission to grant an additional waiver to full time staff where the extra study is of particular relevance to the staff member's job and can be accommodated without detriment to the staff member's work, provided the additional fees waived are met by the staff member's budget centre manager.

Approval Procedures

All staff wishing to claim a tuition fees concession shall complete the application form and submit it to their head of department or section who should forward the application to the Director National Student Administration and Teaching Support Unit by 15 January for first or double semester papers and by 15 June for second semester papers. PhD study may commence at any time.

Payment of approved fees concessions

For eligible staff whose positions are funded through the PIA budget, tuition fees are paid centrally for approved study up to normal limits. Any approved fees concession outside normal limits e.g. for a general staff member to have fees waived for more than 35 points is a charge upon the staff member's budget centre, not the central training budget.

Staff whose fees are not being fully met by the central training budget will receive an invoice. If their budget centre manager has agreed to meet some or all of their fees, they should present the invoice to their manager for payment. Approved tuition fees for eligible staff who are paid through research or other externally funded contracts in department, institutes schools or sections are payable by their budget centre manager from the appropriate non PIA budget. Managers of Full Cost Recovery Centres are expected to pay tuition fees for eligible staff up to normal limits in accordance with University policy.

External Training and Development

University sponsored staff attending external courses From time to time the University may decide to send staff to specific external courses such as the NZ University Administration course. Depending upon the nature of the course and the time frames, nominations may be sought by the Director Training and Development from appropriate managers. Representation will be decided by the Nominations sub committee of the Training and Development Advisory Committee in accordance with the criteria outlined below. Fees (and approved travel and accommodation where applicable) will generally be met from the centralised training budget. Any other incidental costs are the responsibility of the nominating department or section. Staff members supported from this budget are generally expected to submit a brief report to the Director, TDU, and, where appropriate, may be expected to pass on the knowledge and skills gained to a wider group, for example through seminars or workshops.

Criteria for the selection of individuals.

Criteria are as follows.

Likely benefits (in relation to cost) to the University from that person's attendance;

The individual's previous and likely future contribution to the University;

The individual's demonstrated commitment to professional development;

The amount of support already provided to that department;

Meeting the special training and development needs of minority groups within the University in accordance with the University's Charter; and other criteria determined from time to time by the Training and Development Advisory Committee.

Staff Sponsored within a College or Division

Staff may be granted permission to study for external qualifications relevant to their employment in accordance with the terms of the applicable employment contract. Heads of departments or sections may also grant staff permission to attend external courses not leading to formal qualifications where these are of immediate relevance to their position and not available within the University.

Budget centre managers may agree to meet some or all of the tuition and travel costs incurred. Staff whose salaries are not paid from the PIA budget should not have the costs of external training paid from that budget but may be supported from other appropriate sources. Staff of the Training and Development Unit can advise upon external courses.

Reimbursement of fees for approved external study

Staff who wish to claim reimbursement of fees in accordance with the terms of the applicable contract of employment must obtain prior approval for the course of study from their head of department and submit receipts and evidence of success when making a claim. New Zealand Vice Chancellors' Committee Triennial Inter University Conferences of Teachers in each Discipline Meetings of University teachers in each discipline may be held triennially, taking place whenever possible either immediately preceding or immediately following other meetings of the subject concerned.

The expenses for travel and accommodation for up to three teachers from each participating university shall be aggregated and then shared by the participating universities in proportion to the numbers of participants who attend from each university. No funds are available from the Vice Chancellors' Committee.

In the case of Inter University Conference of Modern Language Teachers, the expenses for travel and accommodation for one teacher for each language (where more than three languages are taught) or for up to three teachers (where three or fewer are taught) from each participating university shall be aggregated and then shared by the participating universities in proportion to the number of participants who attend from each university. No funds are available from the Vice Chancellors' Committee.

Any University wishing to send additional teachers may do so. The actual cost of sending additional teachers must be met in full by the teacher's own university, in addition to meeting an appropriate proportion of the shared costs as calculated in terms of paragraph 2 above. Each Conference must be approved by the Vice Chancellors' Committee and approval must be sought in the year preceding the proposed Conference.

A list of participants and a brief report on the Conference is to be submitted to the Vice Chancellors' Committee by the organising Professor. The organising Professor's University shall be responsible for administering the sharing of costs among the universities. When a conference is approved, universities will be advised of the date and place of the conference, together with the name of the organising Professor. Wherever possible, conference must be held at a University, during vacations, and utilising university residential accommodation.

The length of conference shall be up to a maximum of three days (two nights). Costs will be on the basis of transport, plus maintenance at the rate as approved by the NZ Vice Chancellors' Committee from time to time. The primary purpose of the meetings is discussion of academic administration problems, such as curricular developments, course structures, teaching, examining and assessing, transfer of credits, and relations with other educational institutions. The Vice Chancellors' Committee expects to be informed of areas in which co operation and co ordination are required to prevent undesirable duplication in the development of new courses, or to promote the more efficient use of the resources of the university system in existing courses. Any costs in excess of the authorised shared costs will remain as a charge against the departmental travel allocation. The additional costs will comprise.

the expenses incurred by the (up to) three representatives in excess of the foregoing formula;

the expenses of any additional persons attending the conference.

Expenses, Massey Procedure

The NZ Vice Chancellors' Committee authorises the holding of inter university subject conferences from time to time. These are held at intervals of not less than three years. The following financial provisions apply. The costs of up to three representatives from each University will be shared among the Universities in proportion to the number of representatives (up to three) from each. The maximum amount which may be included in the cost sharing comprises.

travel costs mainly airfares

daily allowance as determined by the Vice Chancellors' Committee from time to time for not more than two days.

the number of representatives under the formula;

the venue of the conference.

An adjustment by way of refund or additional payment will be made when total costs have been allocated).

The University will meet the expenses payable under the cost sharing arrangement from a travel fund set aside for the purpose. As these costs have been met from departmental travel allocations in the past, some adjustment will be made to future travel allocations to those departments which have these conferences. Any costs in excess of the authorised shared costs will remain as a charge against the departmental travel allocation. The additional costs will comprise.

the expenses incurred by the (up to) three representatives in excess of the foregoing formula;

the expenses of any additional persons attending the conference.

Normal rules apply to travel to these conferences, e.g. the prior approval of the employee's Manager is necessary, the money allocated for departmental travel must not be overspent, normal fares and subsistence limits apply, where a lesser rate is deemed appropriate by the Manager this should be applied or a grant in aid approved.

8

Training Education and Development Policy

Assurance Statement

The Training, Education & Development Policy aims to provide a flexible framework that will enable managers to maximise the skills & abilities of their staff to deliver the diverse range of modernised mental health services within the Trust.

Introduction

North East London NHS Foundation Trust recognises the importance of investing in the ongoing development of all staff. In turn individual members of staff are expected to make a commitment to develop and apply their knowledge and skills to meet the demands of their post and to work flexibly in the interests of the service. The Training, Education & Development Policy aims to provide a flexible framework that will enable managers to maximise the skills & abilities of their staff to deliver the diverse range of modernised mental health services within the Trust. The policy guidelines are intended to provide fair & equal access for all staff to appropriate development opportunities.

Principles

Learning and development activity should be demonstrably linked to individual learning, training and skills development needs that have been identified through meeting Trust objectives, the Knowledge and Skills Framework (KSF), Personal Development Plans and identified statutory and essential training which have been drawn from national or local requirements which the Trust is required to meet.

Managers should ask the questions.

Why is the member of staff engaging in the development.

How will the development assist in meeting individual, team and organisation objectives.

What should the outcomes of the development be.

The time and financial allowance guidelines described in section 9 must be operated with fairness and sensitivity across all areas of the organisation.

Aims and Objectives

The policy guidelines are intended to provide fair & equal access for all staff to appropriate development opportunities. .

- To maximise the skills and abilities of staff
- To ensure compliance with statutory and mandatory training
- To comply with the relevant criteria in Standards for Better Health and The Clinical Negligence Scheme for Trusts (CNST)

Duties and Responsibilities

The Trust recognises the significant contribution that

users, carers and Trade Union Learning Representatives can make to the development of our staffs' skills and will work closely with representatives to ensure this partnership is effective. Managers will encourage their staff to give consideration to their learning needs, enable them to take personal ownership and share the responsibility for meeting them.

Managers will be expected to view staff development as essential to the delivery of an excellent service and must ensure protected time for staff to acquire appropriate skills.

Developing a Learning Organisation

The Trust will encourage and support the multi professional, multi agency approach to developing further skills and knowledge in our staff. Continuous feedback through regular supervision and appraisal is encouraged for all staff to enable them to be supported in achieving the highest standards in their roles.

The Trust, through the development of the Knowledge and Skills Framework Personal Development Plans and the introduction of e ksf, will work towards all managers and supervisors being equipped to support staff development. The Trust will work towards a positive environment and culture where learning is a positive sign of high performance and growth and not a failure or weakness. The Trust is committed to protected time for staff development and there is a mutual responsibility to make effective use of this time.

Emphasis should be placed upon the most appropriate and cost effective solutions to developing an individual's knowledge, skills and abilities. Attending development/ training programmes, although a popular choice, may not always be the most appropriate method. Learning & development specialists, within the Human Resources Directorate, will provide guidance to managers in exploring suitable options for the development of their staff, which may include work based development opportunities and e learning.

Access to and support for development must be based upon a jointly agreed and structured planning process that relates to the individual's KSF outline, team and organisational requirements. Such development needs should be related to past present performance and the future demands of the role. Personal Development Plans should be fluid and responsive plans, which state learning needs, action required to achieve learning and dates of expected achievement.

A copy of the Personal Development Plan will be held by the individual staff member who is expected to take responsibility, with support from his her manager, for actioning the Personal Development Plan.

The Development Review Process

The development review is an ongoing cycle of review, planning, development and evaluation for individuals against the demands of their post (as described in the NHS KSF outline for that post). All staff in the NHS who come under Agenda for Change will have an annual NHS KSF development review. The development review process has four stages.

a joint review between the individual and their reviewer (line manager or another person acting in that capacity) of the individual's work against the demands of their post.

The production of a Personal Development Plan (PDP) which identifies the individual's learning and development needs and interests. The plan is jointly agreed between the individual and their reviewer and should be linked to the agreed objectives of the individual and the team, plus the career aspirations of the person

learning and development by the individual, support by their reviewer.

an evaluation of the learning and development that has taken place and how it has been applied by the individual in their work.

The cycle then starts at again.

The main purpose of the development review is to look at the way in which an individual member of staff is developing in relation to.

* the duties and responsibilities of their post and current agreed objectives
* the application of knowledge and skills within the workplace
* the consequent development needs of an individual member of staff.

It is expected that reviewers will have regular informal discussions with individual staff members throughout the year, providing constructive feedback on the individual's work and related development. The development review is an opportunity to think about this in a structured way.

If any issues are identified in the individual's work or development during the year, these should be addressed at the time they arise, they should not be left until the review meeting. Any disciplinary issues must be dealt with through the normal channels. The guiding principle of the development review process is "no surprises". The Trust's first priority is to make adequate provision for the training requirements identified to meet statutory and mandatory responsibilities in health & safety and risk management.

All other learning and development will be prioritised by the manager in line with individual personal development plans. When considering individual and team development, affordability assessment should include.

- Time release
- Replacement costs
- Course seminar expenses
- Travel & subsistence expenses

Guidelines for Entitlements

Whilst it is recognised that any development will be of benefit to an individual, there are categories of training which require different considerations.

Option One

Statutory Training is that which is a legal requirement to attend. Mandatory training is that considered by the Trust as essential to the safe performance of person's role and, as such, is an essential Trust requirement.

Option Two

'Mutual benefit' development aims to further enhance the knowledge and skills to the benefit of individuals in their current roles, but it is not considered an essential requirement. The Trust will gain benefits from a member of staff performing to consistently high standards and the development would also be viewed as an advantage to the individual's future career path.

Option Three

Career Development external to role relates to any training and development, which is not directly required and which may assist any future progression or career that a member of staff may wish to embark upon.

Time & Financial Allowance Guidelines

Whilst the following guidelines are for managers to

consider as good practice and not prescriptive, it is important to recognise that they are key to providing a fair, equitable and consistent approach across the Trust. As such, managers should be clear about their reasons in cases were the guidelines are not followed. The Appendix is an 'at a glance' referral to guidelines. It is important to stress, under option 3, that time allowance is at the manager's own discretion and dependent upon any identified service need priority.

Study Leave Forms

All training activities should be agreed between the Line Manager and the individual and linked to the personal development plan. Training must be approved by the Line Manager and a completed study leave form forwarded to the Human Resources Development department. All study leave forms must be sent to the Human Resources Development Department for reporting and audit purposes.

Monitoring reports are produced for the Trust Board, Health Care Commission, CNST and for planning training and development for the future.

The Strategic Workforce Development Group

The Strategic Workforce Development Group is accountable to the Integrated Governance Committee. The Strategic Workforce Development Group is the strategic monitoring and ratifying group for corporate training and development within the Trust, ensuring that training and development is in line with service development.

The functions of the Group are to.

- ratify training and education contracts and commissions across the Trust.
- commission pre & post registration training.
- monitor and evaluate the Corporate Training

Education and Development plan.

- ensure best value is being gained from all available funding sources.

This group holds ratifying power for all development the Trust wishes to undertake in line with the workforce strategy.

Locum and Agency Staff Access to Training and Development

Long term medical staff have access to the consultant appraisal process. Any long term locum agency staff, working as part of a team, will be given access to any 'team' development that is undertaken. All locum and agency staff would be expected to attend fire training and any other statutory training directly related to health and safety, as determined by local manager. Allied Health Professional locum staff may access development and training opportunities at the discretion of their manager, if the employing agency agrees to fund the time and either all or a proportion of the cost. Training for temporary staff working for NHS Professionals will be funded as part of the overhead charges to the Trust.

Process of Implementation

The policy will be launched via Trust Intranet and the website. The policy will constitute part of the Human Resources Development's slot during Corporate Induction events.

Monitoring Arrangements

All training and development activities across the Trust will be captured, monitored and evaluated by using the AT Learning Management system. Non attendance will be followed up and reported in performance reports. Records will be kept of all training attended. The records will be monitored to ensure equity of access and regular reports produced. The Learning & Development Manager will be responsible for monitoring key areas. Director of Human Resources & Organisational Development will be responsible for the overall monitoring of the Policy and Procedures.

Equality Statement

The North East London NHS Foundation Trust is committed to providing appropriate training education and development opportunities for all staff, regardless of age, race, gender, sexual orientation, hours of work, marital status, disability or religion.

The policy enables managers to work within a flexible framework of guidelines that support fair & equitable access to development opportunities derived from an individual personal development plan and the team and Trust's requirements.

9

Civil Service Training and Development Strategy

As Commissioners with responsibility for upholding the principle of appointments to the NICS being on merit on the basis of fair and open competition, we are committed to continuing our own professional development and to getting the best from those who support us in our functions. To this end, we will ensure that the Chairperson and Commissioners continue to receive appropriate and relevant training and development to enable us to carry out our role and responsibilities effectively. The Commissioners also have responsibility to hear appeals to them by civil servants under the NICS Code of Ethics, and may under the new Code consider taking complaints directly. Commissioners' expertise is regularly updated and refreshed. We have again endorsed this as a priority with recruitment training being refreshed on an annual basis, taking account of any new legislation which impacts on our role. Relevant training and development is also made available for those who provide us with support. In the latter context, there is a responsibility on each member of the secretariat to identify his or her perceived training and development needs, and to discuss these with their line manager.

Business Context

The Commissioners' Business Plan for 2007 08 and the

Communications Strategy set out the Commissioners' objectives and targets for the year ahead. This Training and Development Strategy supports the achievement of these objectives and targets. In 2007 08, development and training will therefore focus on.

Organisational Learning and Growth.

- To provide effective strategic leadership and direction to the OCSC secretariat
- To provide training and continuous professional development for the Commissioners
- To maintain a well managed, trained and motivated secretariat

Customers.

- To promote public confidence in recruitment to the NICS To provide timely responses to queries from the Public and Ministers
- To provide timely and appropriate advice to NICS Department NIO on interpretation of the Recruitment Code remit of Commissioners
- To approve SCS appointments within the specified timescales To progress Code of Ethics appeals by civil servants with minimum delay
- To promote equality of opportunity and good relations duties under Section 75 of the Northern Ireland Act 1998
- To demonstrate our commitment to freedom of information

Processes.

- To ensure the Commissioners have effective support and advice to enable the achievement of their statutory role and responsibilities

- To effectively and efficiently manage Commissioners' meetings with the support of the secretariat
- To support and assist the Chairperson and Commissioners in developing their role
- To produce an Annual Report on time To effectively audit NICS recruitment practices against the new Recruitment Code and complete an agreed audit programme
- To continually review processes for improvement including electronic records management
- To monitor and report on exceptions to the merit principle To keep the website up to date
- To evaluate key outputs as appropriate

Resources

- To maintain staffing levels required for the effective discharge of the Commissioners' functions
- To deploy and manage resources to secure good value for money

Training and Development Priorities For 2007 2008

Top priority in training and development is to ensure that everyone is capable of carrying out their responsibilities to the best of their ability and in a manner which aspires to excellence in terms of quality, relevance, timeliness and accuracy of service provided. Such a service will be provided best by people who are clear about their role and what is expected from them by way of individual and collective contribution. Our Business Priorities for 2007 08 are set out in a statement by the Chair and the Business Plan sets out in detail our work objectives and targets for 2007 08. Both of these documents are available on our website.

The NIO Strategic Learning and Development Priorities 2007 08 200 09 have been taken into account in developing this Strategy. The priority for the Commissioners is that they provide strong leadership and direction for all aspects of the process of recruitment to the NICS, emphasising the significance of securing equality of opportunity, fairness, transparency and diversity. The outcome will be a civil service which enjoys the support and confidence of the public and which reflects the composition of the community at large.

The independence and objectivity of the Commissioners are also vital to their role of hearing appeals under the NICS Code of Ethics. For the secretariat, the Business Plan, Job Descriptions, Forward Job Plans and regular opportunities for discussion with line managers, will enable all our support staff to understand what they are doing, why they are doing it and for whom they are doing it. Line managers are best placed to help explain the role of the Commissioners and to help staff identify their training and development needs as they seek to provide support. These needs will be incorporated in individual Personal Development Plans. The introduction of a new appraisal process based on Professional Skills for Government will be monitored and all staff will receive appropriate training in the new arrangements.

All Commissioners and line managers will be encouraged to set an example in leadership and to help staff to feel valued by ensuring that.

- staff are kept fully informed about the Commissioners' Business Plan and Communications Strategy;
- each member of staff has a job description, a forward

job plan and a personal development plan;

- team meetings are held regularly to review work plans;
- the performance appraisal cycle, including half year reviews, is used to take stock of such arrangements and to assess each individual's contribution; and
- annual reports are completed on time.

Training and development will be delivered in a variety of ways ranging from learning on the job or participation in events of general application through to specific courses, tailored to a particular purpose.

The training priorities for 2007 08 are.

- all Commissioners will be thoroughly equipped to provide professional, independent and objective leadership in chairing Senior Civil Service recruitment panels;
- all Commissioners and staff will be aware of business and communication priorities and kept abreast of relevant information, especially that emerging from relevant bodies such as the GB and RoI Commissioners, Equality and Human Rights bodies, Cabinet Office, DFP and other relevant sources;
- all new staff will receive induction training and on going training on the Commissioners' role and individual activities as appropriate, which enable them to promulgate the role and activities to key stakeholders;
- Commissioners will receive refresher training on the management of the recruitment process;
- specific information sessions on new, relevant

legislation and recruitment methodologies;

- Commissioners will receive training in investigative techniques including liaison with other bodies which deal with complaints, as necessary, for the purposes of effective handling of appeals under the Code of Ethics;
- Commissioners will arrange information and sharing sessions with other Commissions and Commissioners;
- equal opportunities and health and safety training will be provided as appropriate;
- awareness education and training in areas such as human rights, equality and diversity will be provided as appropriate;
- for all secretariat staff, training in the new appraisal process and, especially for line managers, advice and help in drawing up job descriptions, forward job plans and personal development plans will be available;
- all secretariat staff, and especially line managers, will be given advice and help in evaluating training and assessing its usefulness both to the individual and to their role in supporting the Commissioners;
- training in leadership, corporacy and management skills will be available for all line managers;
- line managers will be provided, as appropriate, with training in setting business objectives, targets and evaluation techniques;
- for all staff, training will be available in communication skills, customer service and relationships. This will include the organising and

arranging of meetings and events, management of diaries, minute taking and implementation of the Communications Strategy action plan;

- training in financial management and awareness will be available to all staff;
- all staff will be encouraged and trained, as appropriate, to make greater use of information technology and to be proficient in the use of Oasis3 technology for the management of information;
- other specific tailored or customised training will be provided as required.

The return of devolution could have a significant impact on the Commissioners and the secretariat if, for example, the function was moved from the "reserved" to the "transferred" field. This would involve a new relationship for the Commissioners with the devolved administration), a new arrangement for resourcing the function and a structural change for the secretariat. The expectation is that it would also have an impact on the volume of work required in relation to briefing and awareness sessions for Ministers, Departmental Committees and political parties.

Civil Service Reform and continuing political developments, in particular any proposed restructuring of Departments, will be reviewed regularly to ensure that the Commissioners and the secretariat are ready to respond to changing circumstances. Commissioners will wish to ensure that their independence and objectivity is recognised and valued, and that they can continue to operate in a politically neutral environment. Other developments, such as the "HR Connect" process and RPA implementation, will also be closely monitored as these are likely to require some adjustments to working practices and relationships. Commissioners will wish to be regularly appraised of progress and take steps to ensure that there is no compromise or dilution of their existing role or mandate. We have identified clarification of respective roles as a priority during 2007 08.

Evaluation

Training and development is expected to lead to a number of improvements. With regard to staff in the secretariat, an evaluation of all training and development received will be carried out post event and reviewed in year with the line manager. An assessment will be made of the expected benefits of training and development activities and an evaluation will be undertaken at an appropriate time thereafter to ascertain whether the anticipated benefits have accrued.

Training stages

The training activity will develop according to the following four training stages which the skill units refer back to.

"Training of Trainers", will provide the participants with concrete instruments for professionally planning and providing training processes. Moreover, in these phases the students will be oriented toward the issues concerning tourists with special needs,the role and operational area of the professional figure and will acquire basic knowledge about safety in the workplace.

"The tourism system", intends to offer a precise and detailed outline of the characteristic features of the tourism scenario, in such a way that it includes at least a general outline of its functioning and of the tourism distribution processes.

"The trainer of tourism for all", is aimed at providing participants with the knowledge about the topics of the accessibility of the tourism product necessary for carrying out the professional activity of specialised training on the topic of tourism for all.

"Project Works", during this phase the course participants will put the skills acquired in the classroom into practice and will themselves develop training modules (Project Works) on the topics of the accessibility of the tourism product, of welcoming disabled clients and of the preparation of products suitable for the target identified, which they will dispense themselves in the subsequent experimentation phase foreseen in the project.

During the training programme, there will be two intermediate tests of approximately two hours each. The first test will evaluate the degree of learning of the topics dealt with during the first two stages of training; the second will verify the degree of learning of the topics of the third training phase.

10

Role and Responsibilities Identitying Training and Development

---

Ideas And Information

Rule ideas 'in' rather than ruling them out straight away; you never know. Give ideas to smaller groups to work on and test more intensively. Allow time for people to get information and keep a good record of all the ideas suggested, the discussions about each one and why they were either accepted and implemented or rejected.

Decisions

A decision supported by all is better than one imposed on the group or accepted only by a majority (or even a minority!). It's unlikely that all decisions will satisfy everyone, so be prepared to compromise from time to time. Ensure that people who don't support the decision will go along with it. Clarify who is doing what and that all tasks are properly defined.

Evaluate

Once a decision has been put into effect, how it has been implemented, whether the decision had the effect intended and its cost effectiveness will need to be evaluated and reviewed. A useful framework used widely in the voluntary sector is DECIDE.

Define

Groups need to clearly define the situation and limit discussion to just that topic, without letting new issues or 'red herrings' muddy the waters. They need to control the process of definition and make sure everyone is 'signed up' to the process. They must also decide who needs to be involved in the process, how long it should take or be allowed to go on and what is needed for a good decision to be made.

Exploring

A good way to disrupt the unity of the group is for one person or a smaller group to define the problem and produce pre prepared proposals or solutions that people aren't ready for. The group needs time and space to explore problems and solutions.

Clarifying

To remain engaged and to ensure that decisions once made get implemented properly, everyone needs the appropriate information and needs to understand it and the implications of what's been decided.

We may have no or limited experience of team working. Or we may work in a group in ways that are inappropriate for a new project we are planning. We need a framework for working together and deciding things that can help team working no matter what the situation.

The Sector

Knowledge of other local social enterprises Ability to identify opportunities Knowledge of funding sources Experience of making funding bids Experience of assessing funding bids.

Existing Skill Required Skill

Legal Knowledge

Legal responsibilities of committees
How charities work
Responsibilities when employing someone
Leases and contracts

Financial Skills

How to read an income and expenditure account
How to present financial information
How to prepare a budget
Preparing a cashflow forecast
Preparing a profit and loss forecast
How to keep simple accounts
Doing the payroll

Personal Skills

Confident in your abilities
Ability to understand complex issues
Ability to see pros and cons of a proposal
Willingness to question people's assumptions
Ability to assess risk/understand implications
Good at listening
Able to say what you think
Taking the lead/being a leader
Dealing with authority

TRAINING NEEDS ANALYSIS

List any training or experience relevant to your work, including short courses attended.

Rate Your Skills

Circle the number closest to your skill level.

My publicity marketing skills
Organisation's publicity marketing skills

My financial skills
Organisation's financial skills
Your ability to deal with people
Organisation's ability to deal with people
Your ability to do your assigned job
Your ability to do the job you would like
Your ability to work with others
Organisation's ability to manage people

Joint Agreement on the Guidelines for the Training and Development of Development of Employees in Further Education College

Objectives

All employees should have the right of access to training and development support provided by colleges. No category of employee shall be treated less favourably and denied access to training and development support purely with regard the terms of their contract of employment or any act, or deliberate failure to act, of the employer. Both sides recognise and value the contribution of training and development for all employees in further education colleges as a means of facilitating the deployment of employees' knowledge, skills and experience in their personal and the college's development to help achieve personal and organisational objectives.

In particular it is recognised that an effective training and development policy can be a crucial factor in addressing inequalities in employment in relation to race, gender and disabilities. It is recommended that colleges produce a training and development plan, the aim of which shall be to empower all employees to carry out their roles to the highest standards, and deliver high quality services to students. In these guidelines, training and development are broadly defined as those activities aimed at raising the standards of employee practice and thus lifting the quality of the employees' and students' learning and college experiences.

All training and development activities shall be focussed towards the effectiveness of the activities; shall be evaluated in accordance with personal and organisational goals identified via employees' appraisal and the college's strategic plan. These guidelines provide a framework for the provision of training and development support to all employees and will be developed locally with the recognised trade unions.

Section eighteen

These guidelines have been jointly agreed between the trade unions and employers in the National Negotiating Joint Forum. The guidelines constitute a Joint Agreement for the provision of training and development support to all employees in colleges and are recommended by both sides to their constituent memberships.

Training and Development Goals

The types of training and development goals identified will depend on the personal and organisational objectives identified through the strategic planning process and the agreed appraisal procedure. In any event the goals shall, as a minimum standard, take account of the following.

- The Mission
- The Values
- The strategic objectives of the college
- Equal Opportunities Policy
- Requirements for core competencies
- Continuing personal and professional development
- Requirements for professional and vocational

qualifications in further education

- Requirements for professional, vocational and workplace updating
- Requirements for organisational change
- The operational objectives of the school faculties department units
- Operational performance requirements
- Personal performance requirements
- Team performance requirements
- Self assessment and action planning

Consultation

Consultation should take place with recognised trade unions every six months on the evaluation of training and development activities undertaken in the preceding six month period and in respect of proposed training and development activities for the forthcoming six month period. This requirement complies with the statutory provisions of the Employment Relations Act 1999.

11

Types of Training and Development Support

All employees shall have access to the staff development programme in place in the college. They shall also have the full opportunity to attend courses and conferences to develop their professional expertise relevant to the fulfilment of the requirements of their job. The induction procedures shall be fully integrated into the training and development programme for new employees. The agreed Appraisal Scheme within the college shall be applied equally to all employees. All employees shall be given opportunities to attend meetings to the fulfilment for the requirements of their job, e.g. team meeting and course development meetings.

Managers shall endeavour to arrange such meetings at times, which are mutually convenient to all employees. Attendance outside of the contractual terms will be paid at the appropriate rate or as TOIL. There should be clear procedures whereby employees may apply for training and development opportunities, and are given clear reasons for the acceptance or rejection of their applications.

Workplace Learning

All employees shall be encouraged to learn regularly and rigorously from their workplace activities and share their learning experiences and outcomes with their peers. Mentoring of new, existing employees and job changers is recognised as a valuable means of achieving shared workplace experience and promoting excellence in the workplace.

Values

The implementation of these guidelines should seek to encourage an organisational culture in which learning thrives. Both sides recognise that high quality and appropriate training opportunities support the achievement of the colleges' strategic objectives and empower employees to achieve high standards.

Training and Development Activities

The training and development programme for each year should, wherever reasonably practicable, be scheduled flexibly to accommodate the working patterns of all employees, to allow them to undertake activities during their normal contracted working hours.It is recommended that colleges should identify annually a set budget for training and development and set a number of days for personal and cross college training and development activities.

The planning of the training and development activities will be subject to consultation with recognised trade unions. Individual employees of the college should also be encouraged to participate in the consultation on the proposals for the provision of training and development activities for the forthcoming year. A review of each individual employee's training and development activities should be carried out annually via the college's agreed Appraisal Scheme, and periodically throughout the year, as required by the apppraisee and the appraiser.

The colleges' professional and occupational training & development activities for their employees should be mapped against relevant standards, for example FENTO, other NTOs or professional bodies and DfEE requirements in relation to professional qualifications. The standards should inform appraisal, providing criteria against which employees can analyse their skills and strengths, and their learning and training needs in relation to their professional and occupational responsibilities and goals.

Sharing Best Practice

Sharing best practice within and beyond an individual college is recognised as a cost effective way of maximising the value added that can be achieved from training and development activities. Numerous opportunities exist within colleges, including staff meetings, bulletins, classroom and workplace observation, work shadowing.

The FEFC LSC managed Standards Fund opportunities for colleges to share good practice with colleagues in other colleges should be maximised to develop the following activities.

- Inter college 'inspection' teams
- Inter college bench marking
- Collaborative workshops and seminars
- Exchange

Evaluation

The implementation of the college's training and development plan will be monitored and evaluated against clear criteria. The results of the evaluation should be available to all staff and to recognised trade unions and will inform the next training and development planning cycle. Particular care should be taken in the monitoring and evaluation process to ensure that there is no discrimination on the grounds of gender, race or disability, and that all staff, full or part time, have equal access to training and development opportunities.

Implementation

The guidance set out in this Joint Agreement on Guidelines is recommended to Corporations. Both sides recognise the guidelines of this Agreement fulfil the requirements of the Employment Relations Act 1999 in respect of consultation with recognised trade unions. The principles of this Agreement in respect of access to training and development opportunities shall be commended to employment agencies and third party providers engaged by colleges.

Interpretation, Monitoring and Review

The interpretation of any aspect of this Agreement may be referred to the Joint Secretaries of the National Joint Forum for comment and advice. This Agreement will be subject to regular monitoring and review and any amendment will be, by agreement, within the National Joint Forum.

A Training and Development Strategy for the North Western Synod

Preamble

When in October 2002 Philip Wood gave notice of his resignation as Mission Development Worker the Mission Executive asked a small group to consider future options and to produce, through the Training Committee, proposals for an overall Synod Training Strategy which could be offered to the October 2003 meeting of the Synod. This was reported to the March 2003 meeting of the Synod at which opportunity was taken through the use of a questionnaire to consult with Synod members.

At the initial request of the Mission Executive and with the commendation of the Training Committee, Susan

Armitage, Peter Brain, Brian Jolly and George Morton, in consultation with Leo Roberts and Martin Truscott, produced the first draft of this paper. The Training Committee is now pleased to offer this paper in its final form to Synod for consideration.

Recent and existing resources

At present the Synod benefits from the services of a full time Youth and Children's Work Training and Development Officer and a half time Ministerial Training Officer. Until the end of January 2003 the Synod employed, in addition, a full time Mission Development Worker. Alongside these paid staff there are other people (ministers and elders) who facilitate a variety of training and mission development opportunities within the Synod.

The Synod has been served by a full time Youth and Children's Work Training and Development Officer (funded largely by the central church) since 1995. Leo Roberts' main duties are to provide training and support for individuals, local churches and District Councils in their work with children and young people.

The half time post of Ministerial Training Officer was created by the Synod in 1999. Martin Truscott's primary responsibilities are to advocate and administer the central church Post Ordination Education and Training and Continuing Ministerial Education programmes within the Synod.

A full time Mission Development Worker was employed during the period February 2000 January 2003. Areas of work attributed to the post (for example, mission audits and training with elders' meetings and pastorates) were undertaken with varying responses from recipients. Much of the fruit expected to grow as a result of this post never materialised; phase one of a particularly important area of work attributed to the post the Local Leaders Training

Programme was successfully completed, but only because of assistance from Dan Muir and others. These disappointments were due largely to a miss match between the post and post holder but also resulted from insufficient planning at the time the post was initiated. The Training Committee believes that the Synod will now benefit from a radical change of approach in the provision of this area of service, and the proposal below provides for this.

Synod consultation

The consultation exercise at the last Synod meeting revealed no surprises. 155 questionnaires were completed, and only one member of Synod responded to the invitation to submit more detailed comments. The conclusion was that the focus of training & development should be on elders, local leaders, ministers and people working with children, and that the primary areas covered should be worship, evangelism, communications and engaging with issues.

Proposal. Training & Development Strategy 2004 2008

Training and development work throughout the Synod will be undertaken principally by.

- Training & Development Officer (youth & children's work) An existing full time post occupied by Leo Roberts
- Training & Development Officer (ministers & church related community workers) An existing half time post occupied by Martin Truscott
- Training & Development Officer (elders & members) A new half time post to be advertised

Oversight and supervision of the Training & Development Officers and the development of the Synod Training and Development Strategy will be the responsibility of the Training Committee. The overall approach will endeavour to be both proactive and responsive to identified needs within the Synod.

The Training & Development Officers will work collaboratively (much more so than in the past), majoring on their specific responsibilities. Their overall responsibility will be to advocate and enable effective training and development to individuals, local churches and District Councils. They will be assisted by others invited by the Training Committee to undertake specific pieces of work.

The major change from past arrangements is in the area of work to be undertaken by the Training & Development Officer (elders & members). The primary role for this new half time post will be to advocate and arrange training and development opportunities for elders (including local leaders) and members; a relatively small amount of time will be devoted to delivery. Resources freed up as a consequence of employing a half time worker in place of a full time worker, together with any other resources Synod devotes, will be used to provide or subsidise a variety of training and development opportunities for elders and members. The Synod is most fortunate to have the Windermere Centre and the Partnership for Theological Education within its boundary and this strategy gives wide opportunity for these valuable URC linked resources, together with other training establishments and opportunities nearby, to be used in new ways for our benefit. It also allows for the arranging of in house events.

The flexibility of the strategy will allow another significant change from the past, in that it will be possible to provide training and development opportunities in which members, elders, ministers and church related community workers can participate together when appropriate. As well as the benefits for those involved, such arrangements are likely to result in economies of scale.

Expenditure relating to the employment and duties of the officers responsible for youth and children's work and ministers and church related community workers does not change as a result of the adoption of this strategy. Expenditure relating to the employment of a half time officer responsible for elders and members will be in the region of £15000 pa (approximately half that of the former full time Mission Development Worker); the funding of training programmes for elders and members has been budgeted at £12000 for 2004 and £15000 for 2005.

Conclusion and Recommendation

The conclusion of the Training Committee is that this strategy will result in a far more versatile, useful and effective provision of training and development opportunities throughout the Synod. The Committee recommends that it be adopted for the period January 2004 December 2008, with a review to be undertaken prior to the March 2008 meeting of the Synod.

Workforce Development and Training Issues

America's human resources are the basis of our innovation capabilities and these underpin our economic strength and national security." Rep. Bart Gordon , Roundtable on the Science and Technology Workforce, June 23, 2005 Workforce training and education is truly an economic development activity, however, it is complicated by the rapid rate of change of science and technology. Coupling this rate of change with the increasingly complex nature of emerging science and technology calls for a new paradigm for educating and training the science and technology workforce.

Today, technologies, like nanotechnology, are so ubiquitous, cutting across many markets with so many applications in a variety of disciplines from energy and medicine to global interoperability. These technologies allow humans the ability to manipulate matter ondemand, instantaneously changing products, services, markets, jobs and supply chains as we know them today. Because of the highly integrative and interrelated nature of these sciences and technologies, traditional education and training methodologies are no longer appropriate to prepare tomorrow's workforce.

Two critical questions need to be resolved to address this dilemma. (1) What will it take for Virginia to maintain global leadership in discovery and innovation in a time of rising international competition in global science and technology enterprise. How can education and training keep pace with the rapid change in science and technology. This paradigm shift will call for a greater collaboration and partnership between educational institutions, business and industry and government. The result will be a more responsive and flexible science and technology training and education infrastructure. Yes, we will still need to prepare traditional scientists, technologists, technicians, and engineers, but ones that have a greater understanding of how science and technology intersect and interact with each other in different environments. This new breed of science and technology workforce must also develop soft skills and an entrepreneurial spirit.

National Trends

Numerous studies have projected science and technology trends that impact the way that future workers need to be educated and trained (National Science and Technology Council, 2004, Electronic Industries Alliance, 2004, Spherion, 2003, National Science Board, 2003 & U.S. Department of Commerce, 2003). All reports call for a comprehensive cradle to grave approach to educating and training tomorrow's science and technology workforce. The reports also acknowledge that the nature of emerging science and technology will demand a more creative and flexible approach to education and training. For example, the National Science and Technology Council's report, The National Nanotechnology Initiative, identified eight cross cutting areas (aerospace, agriculture and food, national defense and homeland security, energy, environmental improvement, information technologies, medicine and health, and transportation and civil infrastructure) of nanotechnology which all have seven common program components.

These seven common program components are necessary in order to properly train and educate future nanotechnologists.

(1) fundamental nanoscale phenomena and processes,

(2) nanomaterials,

(3) nanoscale devices and systems,

(4) instrumentation research, metrology, and standards for nanotechnology,

(5) nanomanufacturing,

(6) major research facilities and instrumentation acquisition, and

(7) societal dimensions.

Whether one works in the nano world of brain machine interfaces, RFID, microphotonics, microfludics, or robot design these core program components provide the foundation for the learning process. These cross cutting or integrative relationships are also very evident in most emerging technologies and all require a good working knowledge of the societal dimensions of science and technology. While biologists, chemists, engineers and the like will always be necessary, others, who not only possess a technical know how but also have the ability to create, analyze, and transform information and to interact effectively with others are needed to fully develop these emerging sciences and technologies. Therefore, new learning environments and curriculum experiences need to be created to best facilitate the learning process. These new learning environments are especially important to providing necessary credential and certification training created by the implementation of a new science or technology.

In order to better understand this impact and need for new training and education strategies and environments, it is import to understand the trends that are driving key areas of science and technology. Top Ten Nanotech Trends for the 21st Century

1. Nanotech enterprises will provide the ultimate convergence of computers, networks, and biotech, and create products never before even imagined.

2. Nano devices invisible, intelligent, and powerful will be used in every industry redefining the limits of what's possible.

3. Nanotech food compilers will create on demand, low cost, quality meals by assembling atoms into food.

4. Smaller than the head of a pin, surgical nanobots will operate from within the human body.

5. Nano biology will prolong life, prevent illness, and increase people's health.

6. Nano enhanced humans will have physical, intellectual, and sensing powers superior to other humans.

7. Nanotech will provide a cheap and available source of energy.

8. Nano factories will build on demand products in an inexpensive, flexible, and rapid process.
9. Nanotech will revolutionize the global economy, providing Power Tools that will produce high tech products with low cost and low tech resources.
10. Nanotech will create new choices that will alter human evolution, raise dramatic ethical issues, and challenge social norms (Canton, 2005).

Similarly, the health care industry provides credence for the need to provide a more integrative education and training process. Like the nanotechnology trends, health care trends will demand a more cross disciplinary knowledge. Top Ten Health Care Trends for the 21st Century

1. Most hospitals, clinics, trauma centers, physicians, and patients will be connected to one large network enabling access to critical medical information.
2. Consumer health information, accessible over a variety of Net channels, will become the most in demand content worldwide.
3. The medical industry will face an ethical and social dilemma over the disclosure of patient information.
4. Health care professionals, available via remote Internet connections, will provide services to millions of people who were previously under served.
5. Medicalbots, nonhuman intelligence agents, will dispense medical care to patients and doctors worldwide to save money and share expertise.
6. Advanced nano biology and genetic technology will eliminate many diseases, accelerate healing, and increase longevity.

7. Bio engineered food will help promote health and longevity.
8. A new generation of smart drugs, implants, and medical devices will enhance our health and performance.
9. Virtual reality medical simulations will become the dominant mode of medical training.
10. Cyber health care that is customized for us designed to monitor, diagnose, educate, and intervene regardless of location or time will be common (Canton, 2005).

Tomorrow's Workforce

The composition of tomorrow's workforce is drastically changing and will create new challenges for science and technology workforce training and education. Unless action is taken immediately the pool of qualified science and technology workers will continue to shrink due to off shoring or lack of people studying or entering science and technology fields. The 77 million boomers eligible for retirement greatly out number younger workers available to replace them. Workers from 25 to 40 years old will decline by 1.7 million by 2008 (Hudson Institute). During the same period of time the replacement pool of 35 to 44 year olds will decline by 15 percent during the same period U.S. Bureau of Labor Statistics. Unlike workers of the industrial age, tomorrow's workers will switch jobs, careers and companies frequently. Thirty nine percent of the workforce now has worked for six or more employers, up from 27 percent in 1999 Spherion's 2003 Emerging Workforce Study. Forty five percent of workers want to change jobs at least every three to five years, up from 26 percent in 1999. Fifty one percent of U.S. workers are extremely likely or very likely to look for a new job or work situation (Spherion's 2003 Emerging Workforce Study). Further compounding future workforce education and training will be the large number of military personnel returning to the civilian workforce. Therefore, science and technology education and training must be made attractive to the K 12, university, and military generation that grew up with computer games. At the same time it must be adaptive and flexible enough to train and educate low skilled adults. Education and training must be provided where people work and learn. New compressed formats for learning need to be created that reduce the amount of time the learner spends in instruction, but provide the learner the same content only in a more robust environment. This format could be in traditional laboratories and classrooms, in business and industry through internships, in the home, or virtually anywhere through wireless environments. One such learning environment is that provides an ideal solution for educating and training tomorrow's workforce is practice oriented educational environments.

Practice Oriented Educational Environments

The goal of practice oriented educational environments is to produce educated knowledge workers, people who are equipped not simply with technical know how but also with the ability to create, analyze, and transform information and to interact effectively with others. Practice oriented educational environments align well with integrative curricula, curricula that must remain fluid so that it can be reconfigured as science and technology and the learner's needs change. It is this approach to training and education that can address national critical needs faster and in a more comprehensive way. College is designed as an alternative to the traditional university curriculum for students needing or desiring an affordable third way academic program. Its emphasis on practice oriented learning offers students a contemporary education in select scientific and technical fields, along with development of the personal and professional skills necessary for succeeding in business and industry, and it does so without sacrificing an understanding of the liberal arts and sciences. The key to practiceoriented educational environments is that it is learner centric, custom designed for the individual learner. It also works best in compressed time frames, usually allowing for learners to complete a four year degree in two and one half years. Four key successfully tested educational methods drive this approach.

(1) an integrative and applied curriculum,

(2) web enhanced and other electronic or e learning technologies,

(3) competency based assessment, and

(4) instruction in collaborative and individual professional and personal skills.

Education and training are custom designed for the individual learner using the following guidelines.

1. Electronic education via the Net enables interconnected learning experiences, choices, and opportunities regardless of location.

2. Educational content will be delivered by new computer, interactive TV, satellite, and Internet technologies using interactive online multimedia and multidimensional content.

3. On demand virtual learning will be self paced, self directed, and individualized.

4. Virtual Reality scenarios that depict real world and fantasy experiences will increase the learning impact for all types of education.

5. Real time Net chats with other global learners will make virtual education a satisfying social

experience beyond the limits of time and distance.

6. Teachbots smart agents will transform education, providing personalized guidance when and where people need it.

Harrisonburg Downtown Technology Zone Harrisonburg Innovation Center

The Harrisonburg Innovation Center is the first technology innovation center in the City of Harrisonburg's newly created Harrisonburg Downtown Technology Zone. Located two hours from Washington, D.C. and ideal for federal contractor relocation and technology development, the HIC is a "self networking" environment that integrates intellectual capital with technology to develop health and security solutions for corporate and national well being. The HIC provides client members unprecedented support through their highly developed philosophy and model that networks clientmembers, provides contracting and research vehicles, helps grow client members through business assistance seminars and workshops and provides a "world class" and secure technology infrastructure.

This collaboration between the City of Harrisonburg and James Madison University germinated in the university through student research and was embraced by the City as a means to grow jobs and provide a new economy, one based on technology. The HIC employs a highly sophisticated network model that includes a three tier incentive package; access to university faculty, student interns, and resources, business assistance and mentoring; funding vehicles; and an advanced technology infrastructure with multiple backups. Key for client members is their access to over 4000 university graduates a year. Because of this partnership between the City of Harrisonburg and JMU, HIC clientmembers and their employees have access to customized education and training, designed specifically for their needs. University students have the opportunity to work as interns for client members and serve as part of collaborative research teams. Class projects are also integrated with the work product of the client members. In addition to these educational and training opportunities, the City of Harrisonburg and HIC are working with JMU students and faculty to create a biodiesel and alternative fuels research and production facility. This facility, like the HIC, will provide students with real world educational experiences that will supplement their traditional university experience.

Recently, the City of Harrisonburg, through the HIC, helped facilitate a collaborative between JMU, Visual Link of Winchester and Harrisonburg City Public Schools to establish a program, No Child Left Offline, to provide elementary school children who are on the free or reduced lunch program with computers. This initiative was started as a means to open young minds, which traditionally would never have home access to a computer or the Internet, to the world of the Internet and computing. This program is a way to educate young students beyond the doors of their school, and hopefully get them interested in science and technology at an earlier age.

Synergistic Strategies for Success

In order for training and education to be successful, key synergistic strategies must be in place. These synergistic strategies are.

1. Integrating institutional structures and services Establish links among programs and create pathways that students can navigate to gain necessary skills, credentials and certifications.

2. Accelerating learning Help students learn more, learn faster, and complete programs more quickly.

3. Provide labor market payoffs Help students gain credentials valued by employers, get a first or better job, and advance up career ladders as they gain skills and credentials.

4. Providing comprehensive supports Provide compelling motivators and support systems to help students persist through difficult transition points.

Conclusions

Education and training is a cradle to grave process. With the rapid changes and complex nature of emerging science and technology, new paradigms must to be created at all levels of education and training that better meet the needs of the individual learner. Innovative uses of educational technologies and delivery formats need to be utilized in order to provide real world, integrative learning experiences. Compressed timeframes should also be used that incorporate practice oriented educational environments. Special emphasis should be placed on how to continually provide training and education in national critical needs, especially when special credentials or certifications are necessary. After all, a well trained workforce is the essential ingredient to maintain a competitive advantage in a global economy and provide for a strong national security.

12

Creating a People-centric Organisation – The Role of Training

It is only possible for me to be able to attend this way - 2 years ago we did not have the technology nor the enthusiasm to communicate virtually as such. Today it is a central way of working at Ogilvy and Ogilvyone has piloted what I am now using across our entire Ogilvy organisation. Perhaps it will spark some ideas for you in your roles.

I would also like to thank Angus for taking the majority of the presentation work off our hands, thereby allowing me to help some New Yorkers keep on path.

Agenda and Aims

1. Sharing the Ogilvyone experience
2. Creating the right culture for success
3. Linking personal and business objectives
4. Managing the development and training.

This session will be describing the experience of developing one of the most comprehensive bodies of proprietary knowledge in our industry, marketing and communication services, as well as its distribution through the knowledge management system, and how that is maintained to support the organisation and people in their development and training.

Truffles

The aim of truffles is to support training of people and ongoing management of their work.

Our CFO estimates that we have thousands of people working more productively (and he is one demanding fellow)- we get news to them faster, knowledge to them in usable portions and help to them upon demand. And it happens quickly.

For example, we added a new feature to the site on September 13th. It is called Ogilvy Family Notes. Directly from our top management it distributed and chronicled the news we needed to get around. In photos, memos and video we were able to share the impact of the recent tragedy in a way that our employees found comforting.

Everyday learning accumulates too. One of the things we can definitely say about Ogilvyone is that the kind of work it does for its clients today on the whole is significantly different from what it was doing a few years ago. Some of this is down to changes in the environment, such as the whole development of the internet, but a lot more is also to do with improved thinking and practice in marketing and communications consultancy. For example: today we manage the websites and marketing for 2 of the Top 5 Consulting businesses in the world and another 2 on local bases.

Ogilvyone is also implementing radically more sophisticated international and national relationship marketing services for global brands like IBM. Whilst you cannot give all the credit for that for what Truffles has achieved, there is no doubt that Truffles has shifted peoples practices and contributed to our climate of new thinking, learning and practice that has kept Ogilvyone at the forefront in a changing world.

Ogilvyone Worldwide

Perhaps a small amount of data will help you visualize the challenge we had. Ogilvyone was

- Founded in 1972 by David Ogilvy
- US 2.8 billion dollars in billings
- 116 offices in 55 Countries in 70 Cities
- 4,500 employees including 1,500 interactive specialists
- 12 clients served in 5 or more markets, the number one in the world
- Ranked number 1 in many markets, almost everywhere amongst the top 3.

Ogilvyone is the worlds strongest, most experienced, one to one network. It supports a wide range of clients, from global organisations such as IBM and American Express to national organisations and pro bono serviced charities. It provides these companies with a range of services in the field of communications consulting and the building of infrastructure to support one to one connections between the brand and the customer.

Customer Ownership

Customer Ownership is the brand name of the Ogilvyone proprietary knowledge and practice system that has been developed over the course of ten years. It was designed to support Ogilvyone in enabling people to work smarter.

Customer Ownership began with the process of asking what clients would need and was based on a long-term strategic view, that we will come back to. Today there are 2,305 Creating a People-centric Organisation knowledge objects on Truffles. These vary from documents that have had over 10,000 accesses to those only accessed once.

Customer Ownership was/and is continually developed using knowledge teams of senior people from around the world. Most of these teams brought people from several offices together at once as a task force to develop best practice knowledge. Sometimes drawing on proven experience from around the world, others searching and developing new tools and techniques on behalf of the network. This process was based on the following principles:

- Trying to involve people from different offices so there would be buy-in from those offices later.
- Ensuring that there was involvement and participation by some of the best minds in the network.
- Getting a spirit of ownership in everything that happened.
- Training does not just happen from a centre but also can happen by people training each other across the organisation network.

The role of Stepping Stones, in particular myself, was to facilitate these initial task forces as well as the overall project and on a number of occasions to make significant contributions in terms of thinking and work towards developing the finished products.

12 Principles to Share

Interaction is always better one to one VIPs must sustain responsibility " Grass Tops" alone never make it Practicality matters Be like oysters Every system needs planning and overhauls Discovery online is individual Measure success Visuals are a universal language Workflow is the game of entry, learning path raises the bar

Language cements community Fun matters These are the main principles we have been learning over the last eight years that we have been implementing knowledge management systems. I shall go through them in more detail.

1. Interaction is Always Better One to One

Ogilvyone is a one to one business. This means they help their clients to develop one to one relationships with their customers. They have applied the same principle in the internal way that they operate and in the knowledge management system. Clearly if you can get people to meet face to face there is always a wider range of learning

opportunities available. So the inclusion of e-learning does not exclude the need for face to face meetings. As you can imagine with 116 offices around the world it is not always possible to being together the people that are needed and it is not always easy to share knowledge. That is one of the great advantages of e-learning.

Personalise

We still need to make sure that what people experience is something that they can make personal for themselves. For that reason Truffles, the Ogilvyone knowledge management system, is personalised so that each person can set up their own profile and indicate what their interests are, what communities of interest they want to belong to, and they can store favourites that they would like to look at. They can use this to help them find their way through Truffles and to dialogue with each other in communities of interest around their own initiated topic questions. This is indeed one of the great advantages of an e-learning system.

Create relevance

As a trainer it also means that when documents are loaded on Truffles we can automatically generate personalised communication that tells them that something is on Truffles that they would like to look at. I think this has to be one of the challenges of the e-learning developer: how can you ensure that the design of the system enables learning to be as personalised as possible for its user? Another part of the system is obviously the ability to search through the database and retrieve things that are of interest.

Meet all needs

What this means is that while we support the practice of on and off-line training sessions, we see e-training as a support for self-directed learning. Since the name Truffles derives from David Ogilvy's famous saying. We pursue knowledge the way a pig pursues truffles" , how else could we view it. Truffles is an holistic training concept. Remember, e-training is a way of supporting what used to be called on-the job training as well as formal courses.

We believe in formal course and informal packaging. For that reason we have sponsored the IDM and as Professor

Derek Holder of the IDM who is in the audience will no doubt testify we have broken new ground with them on delivering important content to a larger group of geographically dispersed folks than they would have normally served.

2. Vips Cannot Escape Responsibility

One of the reasons why Truffles has been so successful is because it has had the commitment of the Chairman for over ten years now. When Reimer Thedens, the Chairman of Ogilvyone, kicked off the process of search and development in 1991, he also kicked off his process of commitment to achieving success. This has meant that he has continued to put resources into the project and maintained faith, even when things went less fast than we would have liked and through considerable change, for example the whole development of the web and internet and the new economy issues. At the same time I can also say that it has had the extraordinary commitment of Patty Lyon, originally the Global HR and Training Director and now Knowledge Director. It is all very well for the Chairman to back it, but it also needs hands on executive authority from a senior place to keep the project moving.

Stay the Course on Strategy: Adoption is geometric

If you keep changing your strategy, people get confused. If you continue with your strategy - supporting the knowledge management system - others will come to believe that it is worthwhile. We certainly had times when progress was not as fast as we would have liked.

Organisations that invest in a knowledge management system tend to make a majority of their investment in the system at the beginning of the project. This means there is a temptation to want instant mass take-up of the system and instant returns on the investment. However, our experience shows that it takes a relatively long time for the system to become accepted and widely used, because it involves changes in learning and behaviour patterns. It also takes time for the cynicism to be overcome as well as time for the system to really develop a quality of what is available. For these reasons response is not always instant but what we have found is that once take-up begins it gathers pace throughout the organisation.

One breakthrough can pay for it

At the same time, what we found is that individuals have sometimes had massive breakthroughs and terrific help. We have documented cases where as a result of information people found there is a significant likelihood that they won major pieces of business they might not otherwise have won. Just one of those occurrences could pay for the whole investment.

In Guatemala we won a large banking client because the Office head could demonstrate how quickly information was shared and retrieved-and not necessarily just by industry. In Brazil, we won a major media account after the Office Head spoke at a conference about the power of Truffles. In Germany we recently recruited a senior player, and he attributed the defining acceptance moment on the access he would have to the rest of the network at his fingertips.

Leaders need to lead

Over and above that, it has been really important to get support from the Heads of Office. Not everybody has given an equal level of support and one of the things that has been necessary is to really encourage them to support it within their office. When leaders adopt practices with vision and enthusiasm, then other people follow them. Ogilvyone has a transnational board, its members come from most of the continents of the world and they have also been instrumental in backing it and showing leadership through their contributions in the offices they manage.

For example, Mike Windsor, the President of Ogilvyinteractive worldwide is one of the advocates. Along with creating a special community for interactive developers, he has used our site to communicate with staff. And he also has been a prolific contributor of content. That was especially important because as Head of our e-business his demonstration of belief really counted as a model.

3. "Grass Tops" Alone Never Make It – it needs Grass Roots

The grass roots are of course the heavy user, the people who plunge into the system and draw what is available out of it creating the energy for growth. The Pareto principle operates as much in a knowledge management system as anywhere else. There are heavy users who make extensive use, frequently hours each week, while other people make less frequent use, often accessing only now and again. Partly this is perhaps down to knowledge of what is available, personality and other factors.

Our experience is that you need to identify those who are the heavy users of the system who will make it work, encourage them and they will encourage others to use the system and so the system and its usefulness will grow. For example, they not only ask questions in the discussion zones and but regularly contribute answers and suggestions to what others bring. Obviously we do this by measuring how much people use it and then responding accordingly.

Show recognition

One of the most important contributions Patty makes, and her team around her, is in recognising people and showing appreciation. Often it just needs the social gesture of recognition. But, there may also be career opportunities and it does no harm for people to see that contributions are appreciated. For example, some of them get adopted as local office knowledge managers. Our newest KM in Amsterdam is a senior creative who volunteered for the extra work!

Think global, act local

In each office somebody SENIOR is appointed to be responsible for the system, for encouraging local use, collecting information about likes and dislikes and liasing with the central team in terms of determining the future of the system and encouraging usage:

- E.g, the knowledge manager in Madrid, Spain organised a contest that generated a lot of interest in Truffles and introduced a new generation of users to what was there. It was fun and linked documents and people from around the world.
- Then the idea was picked up in Toronto, Canada.

> The execution was a little different but the rewards were similar-ranging from gourmet nights out to desktop piggie reminders.

It is absolutely essential to make a human connection between the central (or global) team and local users and knowledge managers. One of the ways this is also supported is by having regular web conferences with local knowledge managers as well as meetings with knowledge managers from the major offices, usually twice a year. Our current KM team leader is a Belgian with multicontinent experience. We seek out experts to lead that have ambitions and talent to be truly global.

Engaging advocates and cynics enables you to encourage converts and confront criticism. When you engage cynics in a positive way, they can become advocates and they can also give you many good ideas about things you need to take care of or watch out for as well as things to provide that will enthuse people. At the same time, engaging advocates as we have already said is a way of promoting wide-spread usage.

4. Practicality Matters – training in everything important related to the job

Including simple but useful pieces of information in the knowledge management system, trying to make it as accessible as possible encourages people to visit the site regularly and collect the information they need when they need it. In the process it can also encourage them to investigate other areas of the site. This is the same principle that retailers use.

One of the ways that we do this is that Truffles integrates everything together that Ogilvyone users need. It is not just a separate knowledge management system, related to proprietary techniques and so on, it is the majority of knowledge that people need. It covers all aspects of training from induction into the company, HR practices, names and addresses of people around the globe and so on.

When you register yourself onto the system and give information about yourself, often a combination of fun and chatty stuff with detailed technical knowledge, this is then used to support searches for people with relevant expertise. For example you can find people who work with particular clients around the world. Or you could find out information about people who have specific kinds of expertise. This immediately translates into better work for our clients and a tighter network of people.

Also included are various tools that people can use, for example key templates and spread sheets and also credentials presentation, standard decks for various uses and public information such as press releases.

Altogether Truffles includes all kinds of information such as:

- Cases
- Theory
- Tools
- Discussion Papers and Think Pieces
- Discussion areas where people can exchange views
- Electronic copies of articles from major journals such as the Harvard Business Review and the Interactive Journal
- Speeches
- Sales presentations made to clients
- Examples of work
- And most importantly the best of creative material that has been done with clients around the world.

In terms of induction, we have developed an interactive online tutorial that every employee is prompted to 'take' in their first 3 months with Ogilvy. We call it Ogilvyone

Essentials. As a tutorial it covers the key learning but also enables self-paced learning; in the New York and London offices we combine this with an assigned learning mentor to ensure that people actually turn the course into actionable work everyday. And yes we do reward 2 tiers: completion and excellence!

For example, if as a newcomer you also work on American Express you are required to review a select set of background documents before you may speak with a client anywhere in the world!

Be Like Oysters

Surround yourself with people who make you into a gem. Nobody knows everything and you need to have people around you who can contribute from their expertise in the past and stimulate you in your ongoing journey. For example Ogilvyone worked with Stepping Stones and without their help would probably not have got where we are. We also involved Arthur Anderson in a significant way to help with one step in the process. Plus Ogilvyone has kept in touch with major players like Forrester and others doing research and keeping track of their ideas as well as attending.conferences, as you are on this occasion.

Partnering should always leads to better results. In fact for several years Stepping Stones actually operated as the Ogilvyone knowledge managers. This meant that during a phase when the Ogilvyoners wanted to be focused on researching and developing and other activities, Stepping Stones was responsible for the practical management of the system and the loading of all new material that came into the centre.

Patty: " I suggest we learned from each other. Stepping Stones advanced our ability to deliver what we wished for. And we tried to keep raising the bar to encourage Stepping Stones to bring best in class work to Ogilvy. A small example is our Knowledge Managers Guide (the manual is only a small manifestation of what the Guide includes)-Angus and his team were able to create the framework process before we had the skills to do it.

Literally today we have just issued version 7, and it was created in house. On a larger front, the oyster theme also means that you accept that someone external is not going to be providing

6. Every System Needs Regular Overhauls and Good Planning

The Ogilvyone knowledge management system now has a series of knowledge managers, as I said, one per office, who are responsible for updating the site regularly. We plan a major new release of the system in 2002 as a result of feedback we have been getting over the last couple of years. This is now the third release level we have reached. Our fourth is actually a commercially available product - The Knowledge Refinery. We have had the good fortune to have a service our clients do find is state of the art! (Do ask Patty more about it!)

At the same time what we try to do is put in a version and then stabilise while we get feed back instead of constantly tinkering. That way we put something in, gather feedback about it and then we improve it. Implementing improvements and enhancements also takes a lot of planning and communication. Take what was involved in the launch of Essentials...

Discovery Online is Individual and unpredictable

Everybody learns by themselves. Even when you are in a group of people – the learning needs to take place inside your own head connecting to the system of concepts and associations you already have. It is no different online. What we do is try to enable people to follow their own interests as far as possible. On the one side we provide learning parts that encourage people to go through a series of documents to learn things, on the other we provide general search facilities and so on that enable people just to follow up on their interests. Also, virtually every document is cross-referenced to other documents where there is more information on the same theme. So, as with a good encyclopaedia with crossreferences you can keep following your interest for hour after hour should you have the time and inclination. Moments of Discovery are different for everybody. There fore knowledge breakthroughs are a bit like the chaos theory - somewhat unpredictable. Breakthroughs do not happen everyday - even when that learning is disseminated by e-learning - but an efficient and effective knowledge management system is constructed in such a way that it facilitates these breakthroughs and helps distribute the insights quickly.

Impressions count

The big turn-off turn-on moment is the first visit. Will it deliver value or will it simply confuse? We have designed online communications and help to make this simple. Everyone is welcomed with a small and easy guideinterstitial.

It walks them through registration and help. We then have devised ways to encourage compliancethrough a series of fun filled reminders.

And in the major offices we provide a surprise - a once in a while thank you visit from an Office Head.

Visuals are a Universal Language

In a multilingual environment like Ogilvyone, interesting pictures and good page design enhance the chance of people visiting and using the system. One of the great advantages of Truffles has been the opportunity to distribute a set of standard models and other graphics that people can use around the world so that clients experience consistent and high quality communications and so do the Ogilvyone people.

Design and QA

One of the things that we would certainly recommend is that you pay a lot of attention to the way things look, not only the overall design of the website but the appearance of every document that goes in. The way we do things is that documents can be loaded from any office. But in order for them to go global they have to be approved by one of a number of global knowledge managers. Their job is on the one hand to ensure quality and on the other to take note of good things and make sure they are leveraged and brought to the attention of people who want to know about that particular subject.

Listen

We also allow people to vote. Is the document helpful? The simple mechanism is fast and sends the message that we do want the user's input as well as insights.

9. Measure success

Success needs measurement to make the business case for the future. Things that are not working also need to be discovered and measured so they can be fixed. In Truffles we use many of our own client servicing techniques like Evaluate to help us.

Evaluate required us to assemble a cross-functional and cross continental team that was charged with defining the crucial success points for 2003. From 181 Key Performance Indicators we have been able to identify the driving and relevant metrics. After honing to 18 that we do track, there are measures that our management regularly watch.

Workflow is the Game of Entry: Learning Path Raises the Bar

Which brings me to the point that Truffles as a training path aims to contribute at least two levels:

- It aims to provide tools and techniques that enable people to do what they are doing more efficiently.
- It enables people to think more effectively and therefore operate more effectively in what they do. This goes back to the famous distinction that Peter Drucker made between efficiency and effectiveness: obviously both are needed and Truffles support both. Let me give you an example of what that means. The availability of templates, credentials presentations and other presentations by other Ogilvyoners around the world means that when it comes to doing a new pitch for a client you might well be able to develop a lot of the material a lot more quickly and to a high standard. Now over 60% of the time can be spent in solving a problem rather than reinventing a template. Even more important the way you think about the problems they have and the kinds of solutions you engage with can be an order of magnitude more sophisticated and strategic. People will use the system once they realise that it can help them with their daily work. They will be really enthused about the system when they realise it can transform their daily work.

Language Cements Community

Just as speaking a common language, such as English, can enable people to communicate more effectively so a knowledge management system can help users to speak the language or organisation jargon more effectively giving them an advantage in terms of organisation and efficiency.

13

Strategies for Effective Law Enforcement Training

Introduction

In recent years, law enforcement agencies across the country increasingly have collaborated with community partners to design and implement specialized responses to people with mental illnesses. These agencies work closely with mental health practitioners, people with mental illnesses and their family members, representatives of social service agencies, and others who share their goal of improving the outcomes of encounters with people who have mental illnesses. Their specialized law enforcement-based response programs position officers to safely manage these complex encounters and provide a compassionate response that prioritizes treatment over incarceration when Training: An Essential Element of a Specialized Response Training is one of "essential elements" of any specialized law enforcement-based response program, according to a consensus of experts whose recommendations are captured in the report Improving Responses to People with Mental Illnesses: The Essential Elements of a Specialized Law Enforcement-Based Program (a publication provided with support by the Bureau of Justice Assistance). Reflecting agreement among a broad range of policymakers, practitioners, advocates, and researchers who work on these issues, the Essential Elements report states, "All law enforcement personnel who respond to incidents in which an individual's mental illness appears to be a factor receive training to prepare for these encounters; those in specialized assignments receive more comprehensive training. Dispatchers, call takers, and other individuals in a support role receive training tailored to their needs." To learn more and download a copy of the repor.

Strategies for Effective Law EnforcementTraining appropriate. While variation exists among agencies with these programs, they share a common feature: officers who respond to incidents involving a person with a mental illness receive extensive training for this role.

Training enables law enforcement personnel to perform duties required for an effective response. With training, responders better understand mental illnesses and the impact of those illnesses on individuals, families, and communities. They are also better prepared to identify signs and symptoms of mental illnesses; utilize a range of stabilization and de-escalation techniques; and act in full awareness of disposition options, community resources, and legal issues, all of which vary by jurisdiction. Supervisory and support personnel such as midlevel managers, field training officers, call takers, and dispatchers) also receive training that enables them to assist responders and facilitate the specialized program's operations.

While experts agree that training is a core feature of a specialized response program, they also caution that it presents complex challenges. As many practitioners experienced in these law enforcement programs know, training must do more than inform its participants—it must also transform them. To perform effectively in their new role, officers need to acquire a greater understanding of issues and systems with which they may have little familiarity; with this base, they must also master new skills that will enable them to make safe and appropriate decisions during difficult and often tense field encounters. "One of my CIT officers was proud of her ability to calm a person in crisis in her patrol car by turning the radio to an easy listening station.We don't teach that specific tactic, but the CIT training nurtures a level of performance in the field that brings about a change in the culture of police."

Many jurisdictions currently implementing specialized response programs are finding that developing an effective training program is an iterative, time-consuming process that requires patience, commitment, and cooperation among partners. This guide is meant to facilitate this process by sharing lessons from the field, while recognizing that agencies may need to tailor successful strategies from another jurisdiction to meet their unique needs. Personnel who are planning training for a specialized response program can learn much from the experiences of those who have already overcome significant challenges.

This training resource guide is written for law enforcement personnel and staff at other agencies who are planning a training initiative that will support a crisis intervention team, co-response, or other type of specialized law enforcement-based response program, as well as for individuals looking to enhance an existing training initiative. The guide reviews common challenges experienced by several jurisdictions that have developed training for officers encountering people with mental illnesses, and synthesizes the key lessons they learned that could be of benefit to others. To describe these challenges and identify effective strategies for addressing them, the authors conducted field surveys, phone interviews, focus groups, and an analysis of the existing literature on law enforcement training.

The guide will be most useful to stakeholders in jurisdictions that are in the process of developing a training program or want to enhance an existing training effort; the authors hope readers will find it a helpful companion to any training curriculum.3 It considers questions such as which individuals would be most appropriate serving as trainers for this type of effort, how these trainers can be identified, what preparation trainers require, what techniques are most effective, and how planners can achieve maximum impact through these techniques. It is not a "how-to" guide for crafting individual curriculum modules; rather, it provides direction on how to overcome specific challenges that will likely come up during the development or improvement process of most training efforts. In other words, the discussion here focuses less on which topics should be taught and more on how they can be taught most effectively. Several resources are available to assist communities in the critical step of identifying and tailoring curriculum content to address specific jurisdiction characteristics e.g., mental health laws, mental health resources, and law enforcement policies. The process of customizing training to local and

Throughout this document, the term "stakeholders" is used to describe the diverse group of individuals affected by law enforcement encounters with people with mental illnesses, such as criminal justice and mental health professionals; numerous other service providers, including substance abuse treatment counselors and housing professionals; people with mental illnesses and their loved ones; crime victims; and other community representatives.

For a list of potential training topics for coordinators who are in the early stages of curriculum development to consider, see appendix B: Suggested Training Topics.

This guide to training strategies will be most useful for jurisdictions in which a solid foundation for training is in place—in other words, when the following steps have been taken:

- Relevant organization and agency leaders, as well

as other individuals involved in law enforcement encounters with people with mental illnesses, are committed to working together to develop a collaborative response.

- These leaders have formed a multidisciplinary planning committee to discuss all issues related to program planning, including training.
- The planning committee has analyzed their community's problems and available resources to inform the specialized program's policies and practices, which form the basis of the training content.
- The planning committee has determined whether some or all personnel in the law enforcement department should be trained and whether trained officers should respond alone or in combination with mental health providers.
- Agency leaders serving on the planning committee have designated appropriate staff to compose a working group (called a coordination group in this document) responsible for the day-to-day management of personnel training and other program responsibilities. The coordination group, which serves as the administrative body for the training initiative, has determined the length and frequency of training, developed the curriculum, and made key recommendations, such as how to finance training.

The coordination group—members of which are called coordinators throughout this guide—will also oversee identifying and preparing trainers and selecting training techniques. More than any of the other individuals involved in a specialized law enforcement-based response to people with mental illnesses, coordinators are perhaps the group most likely to benefit from the recommendations provided in this guide.

5. The steps outlined here for creating a collaborative foundation for designing and implementing a training initiative are culled from Improving Responses to People with Mental Illnesses: Essential Elements of a Specialized Law Enforcement–Based Program.

6. In addition to the lead law enforcement agency, partners should include mental health service providers and consumers, their family members and loved ones, and advocates. Based on the nature of the problem in the community, additional partners might include other area law enforcement professionals; health and substance abuse treatment providers, housing officials, and other service providers; hospital and emergency room administrators; crime victims; other criminal justice personnel such as prosecutors and jail administrators; elected officials; state, local, and private funders; and select community representatives.

7. In some jurisdictions the planning committee and the coordination group may be the same— particularly in those with small agencies, in rural areas, or with limited resources.

Who's Who in the Training Initiative

A training initiative to improve the lawenforcement response to peoplewith mental illnesses involves experts froma variety of disciplineswho serve a range of functions.To differentiate among the various roles in the training initiative, this guide uses the following terminology:

- Coordinators—Representatives of the law enforcement agency and other stakeholder groups who plan and oversee the training initiative. (Training coordinators often also oversee other administrative aspects in a specialized response program.) Responsibilities include identifying and preparing trainers, designing the curriculum, selecting training techniques, and managing logistics.

- Trainers—Content experts who provide classroom instruction. Trainers can be officers who teach policing functions, mental health professionals who discuss mental health-related topics, other justice or health professionals who explain related legal concerns or substance abuse issues, or community members who describe what it's like to live with a mental illness.

- Role Players—Individuals who perform in the role of a person with a mental illness or another individual who may be involved in the law enforcement encounter during the role play exercise. Role players can come from a variety of backgrounds: they may be professional actors, law enforcement officers, mental health professionals, or consumers.

- Facilitators—Individuals with experience in law enforcement responses to people with mental illnesses who provide instructions and lead debriefing conversations during the role play exercise and other experiential learning activities.

- Participants—Law enforcement officers and other appropriate support personnel who receive training to improve their response to people with mental illnesses. (Because the primary focus of this guide is improving law enforcement responses to people with mental illnesses, recipients of crosstraining other than law enforcement officials—that is, mental health professionals, consumers, and other stakeholders are not included in this category.)

These roles are notmutually exclusive: the coordinatormay also serve as trainer; the facilitator as role player; or the coordinator as trainer, facilitator, and role player.The authors of this guide use specific terms to distinguish among these different functions,while recognizing thatmultiple functions may bewithin a single person's responsibility.

In the mental health system, "consumer" is the term most frequently applied to a person who has received mental health services. The term is sometimes used more generically to refer to anyone who has a diagnosis of a mental illness.

Effective Trainers

Provides strategies for recruiting and selecting the most effective trainers.

Discusses important approaches to teaching content related to mental illness that meet the unique needs of law enforcement personnel and is sensitive to the policing culture.

Effective Training Techniques

Provides guidance on how to use role play exercises effectively, including helping officers to master essential de-escalation techniques.

Illustrates how less traditional law enforcement training options can help officers better appreciate both the difficulties faced by people with mental illnesses and their family members, and the way mental health treatments and supports are provided in their community.

Each chapter lists a set of challenges that jurisdictions have faced in implementing a training initiative, followed by recommendations for and discussions of how they can be addressed.

To ensure that this guide is grounded in practical approaches, it includes experts' words of advice, examples of programs illustrating key themes, and references to supplemental resources.9 Excerpts from the Essential Elements report referenced above are also included to draw the connection between training and key policies and practices that can improve how law enforcement responds to people with mental illnesses.

Effective Trainers

Officers who provide the first response to people with mental illnesses require a broad understanding of relevant issues and a range of skills to perform the unique responsibilities of their assignment. This training should be taught by experts whom officers will find credible. The following sections discuss challenges planners and coordinators often experience

Identifying Trainers Broad Topics, Broad Expertise

Training for law enforcement officers on effective responses to people with mental illnesses must draw on a diverse range of expertise and perspectives to cover a broad range of topics, from recognizing signs of mental illness to understanding the state's emergency evaluation laws. Many of these topics may be better taught by experts from disciplines other than law enforcement. Trainers from the following categories can be helpful in presenting particular topics:

- Law enforcement trainers can provide instruction on all matters related to first response and other policing functions, including officer safety, scene stabilization and de-escalation skills, the need for a specialized response, procedures for transporting an individual to a mental health facility, and the relevance of other agency policies and procedures.

- Mental health practitioners can teach officers to identify signs and symptoms of mental illness and provide information about disposition options and community resources—including advising officers about a drop-off facility's policies and admissions criteria for example, its hours of operation, whether it accepts individuals with co-occurring substance use disorders, and limitations on capacity.
- Consumers and familymembers can provide a face and a voice for people strugglingwithmental illnesses.They can convey to officers the impact ofmental illness on individuals, families, and communities.They are also uniquely qualified to promote a compassionate response fromofficerswho often see peoplewithmental illnesses onlywhen these individuals are in crisis.
- Other criminal justice and health professionals—such as mental health court team members, jail administrators, and emergency room administrators can present relevant legal issues, their interactions with law enforcement, and discuss how the high numbers of people with mental illnesses affect their system.

Effective Trainers

The involvement of particular trainers will largely be determined by the topics selected, the means for presenting them, and the need for more specialized training for individuals who will primarily respond to these calls for service. For example, a department may decide to use an online training resource for ensuring that all officers have a baseline understanding of the signs and symptoms of mental illness but then also bring in mental health professionals to help guide interactive group training sessions for advanced instruction for CIT officers or others acting in a specialized response assignment.

Challenges

- Few law enforcement agencies or their training programs will have the internal capacity or expertise to teach the entire range of topics that first responders require when working with people with mental illnesses.

  Agency training planners or coordinators may also lack familiarity with qualified experts in the community who can adapt material to a law enforcement audience.

- Not all communities will have an adequate pool of local experts who can provide aspects of this training to officers. Planners or coordinators may have additional difficulty identifying outside instructors with expertise in any of the relevant topic areas who have observed a significant number of law enforcement encounters with people with mental illnesses or are familiar with policing culture, policies, and the everyday demands officers face.

- Some agencies will lack the funds to coordinate a training initiative, including expenses related to contracting with trainers.

- Trainers who have had negative encounters whether from the law enforcement or mental health perspective may find that those experiences color their presentations and pose significant barriers to effective teaching, even if the instructors are motivated to help improve law enforcement interactions.

Effective Strategies

☐ Develop in-house expertise to teach law enforcement topics.

If a law enforcement agency is at the beginning stages of implementing a specialized response program, it is unlikely to have personnel prepared to teach policing strategies that are unique to encounters with people with mental illnesses. Relying on outside experts to train all specialized responders or sending all officers to train in other jurisdictions can be costly and may not be as efficient as developing in-house expertise—particularly if this requires significant travel out of the region.

A train-the-trainer course that includes a large number of trainers either from within the agency or along with trainers from nearby agencies— is an ideal way to develop a pool of law enforcement training experts. This course can be taught as a one-time offering by outside experts. Alternatively, an agency can identify officers to serve as training coordinators and send them to another jurisdiction with an active specialized response program

Because the officer, or group of officers, who teaches law enforcement topics will likely become the agency's primary source of authority on this topic, the individuals should have significant experience in patrol and should be respected throughout the agency and community. In many communities, these officers will coordinate the specialized response program and training, represent the agency on the planning committee, and even chair that committee. Work with partners to identify trainers outside the law enforcement agency.

Law enforcement coordinators might not know who would be a good fit to teach modules such as recognizing symptoms of mental illness and strategies for officers to use when mental illness appears to be a factor in the call for service. Training coordinators will need to reach out to respected community partners—especially groups and individuals representing mental health professionals, consumers, and family members—to collaborate on identifying trainers or facilitators.

Members of the training coordination group from diverse disciplines and perspectives should identify individuals who can speak with authority about particular topics. Representatives from mental health agencies can tap their staffs' networks and consult with the local mental health board or relevant faculty at nearby universities for recommendations. Coordinators can also contact nearby jurisdictions to learn whom they have used as trainers.

One of the tougher parts of the training is teaching officers to take a different approach to handling someone who is mentally ill. It is best to have a respected law enforcement officer discuss that portion."

Coordinators may consider conducting training along with other law enforcement agencies in the region to share trainer(s) as well as associated Excerpt from the Essential Elements report "Organizations and individuals representing a wide range of disciplines and perspectives and with a strong interest in improving law enforcement encounters with people with mental illnesses work together in one or more groups to determine the response program's characteristics and guide implementation efforts."

Application to specialized training The coordination group brings together the lead law enforcement agency, mental health service providers and mental health consumers, family members and loved ones, advocates, and other relevant group representatives. It creates a forum for collaborative planning for the training initiative.

Coordinators can work to identify nearby jurisdictions that already conduct regular training sessions on specialized responses and ask if places can be reserved for their personnel. If none are known, coordinators can visit the Criminal Justice/Mental Health Information Network, which is coordinated by the CSG Justice Center and available at www.cjmh-infonet.org. This online network allows users to search for program profiles by state, and provides contact information for each program entry.

Select trainers who have an appreciation for the specialized response program's goals, positive attitudes toward law enforcement, and experience with people with mental illnesses involved with the criminal justice system. Training will be less effective when trainers' past experiences or orientation prompts them to make negative statements about the law enforcement agency or people with mental illnesses.

Some or all members of the coordination group should interview potential trainers to ensure that the instructors' reasons for participating do not run counter to the program's objectives and would not limit their contributions or credibility. Although it may not be practical to conduct a rigorous application process for all potential trainers, it is important that coordinators are aware of trainers' attitudes and level of commitment. When the coordinating group selects family members and consumers to participate in the training, these individuals must be familiar with interactions with law enforcement and have moved beyond any negative outcomes of those encounters. When the agency identifies sworn officers to assist in training as facilitators or in other functions, coordinators should ensure these officers have had sufficient practical experience encountering people with mental illnesses or dealing with crisis situations and likewise are prepared to contribute in a constructive, positive manner.

Effective Trainers

You must be careful to select consumers who have gotten past blaming the police for what happened and can remove themselves from the past. They must be at a point in their recovery to talk openly about their experiences in a way that will benefit the police."

To ensure that trainers are providing core substantive information in a manner that promotes successful learning, coordinators should monitor performance in the classroom. Evaluation can be conducted in a number of ways: coordinators can provide students with evaluation forms, debrief some or all officers informally after the training, or observe trainers in action. This information can be used to determine whether to retain a particular trainer, to provide feedback to enhance performance, or to broaden the search for future trainers.

14

Basic Training Methodology

Introduction

The role of the coach in the development of athletic potential is very interesting and challenging. It is also a very demanding role because it requires knowledge of all aspects of the athlete's life and the requirements of the sport. With this information, you, as the coach, are in a position to prepare a training program that will assist the athlete to achieve his or her training objectives. The training program will provide the format that will guide the athlete through the proper sequence of development throughout his or her athletic career.

The FISA Coaching Development Program provides information in this course on the basic principles of training, the concept of periodization and the development of a training program. This course is intended to provide you with the ability to design and implement simple training programs. Courses to be offered in the FISA CDP Levels II and III will provide more specific information, particularly in regard to the integration of the principal components in the development of athletic potential - the physical, technical and psychological components.

Basic Principles of Training

Basic training methodology has its own principles, which

are based on scientific investigations. These investigations provide guidelines which systematically direct the whole process of training and are known as the principles of training.

Active Participation

The coach and athlete should be active participants in a joint effort to design and implement a training program. This principle is more important with experienced athletes than with beginners since beginners do not possess the knowledge and are subject to the direct control and guidance of the coach. The coach and athlete should develop training objectives and work together in the development of short and long term training programs.

Experienced athletes may be encouraged to develop their own program with the assistance of their coaches to ensure the quality of the program. The coach and athlete should establish tests and standards to be met periodically during the training season in order to monitor and control the effectiveness of the program. This will provide information to assist in the modification of the program during the training season and from season to season.

This active participation will provide a motivating force to enhance the commitment of the athlete and encourage the pursuit of excellence in training.

All-Around Development

All-around physical preparation is an essential part in the development of athletes. In fact, the establishment of a broad base of physical development should be considered a prerequisite for specialization in any sport. This is particularly important for youth and beginners because it is necessary to build a large base of physical fitness and skill to prepare the athlete for the increasing demands of the rowing specific training that will occur as the athlete develops. Although the developing athlete will always maintain an allaround physical preparation program, rowing specific training will become more important both during the training season and from season to season throughout the athlete's career.

Specialization

During the athlete's career, he or she trains with the purpose of specializing in rowing. This specialized training for rowing is necessary given the high level of competition in sport today. This applies to all aspects of training and results in the amount of special rowing exercises being progressively and constantly increased.

Although specialization is a complex process, these special exercises may be divided into two groups. The first group comprises exercises that are similar to the sequence of the movement requirements of the sport (for example, utilization of the rowing ergometer or on the water technical exercises). The second group comprises exercises that represent partial movements of the whole sequence of movements. These exercises activate single or multiple muscle groups in a way similar to the movement requirements of the sport for example, utilization of a strength training program.

Therefore, the development of training programs will present the interesting challenge of properly utilizing exercises for both allaround development and sport specialization while giving consideration to short and long term athletic development.

Individualization

It is necessary to individualize training to enhance the prospects for reaching personal training objectives because of variations in each athlete's ability, potential, characteristics of learning and the specific requirements of rowing. These variations will result in different individual capacities and, therefore, a training program for one athlete may not provide the proper development for another athlete. This realization is particularly important in the event that a programme that has been designed for a senior or experienced athlete is utilized in training a junior or beginning athlete.

The sport of rowing with events for individuals and crews offers the challenge of developing training programs those are both individual and crew specific with consideration also being given to short and long term objectives. This ability is the real art of coaching and is developed after years of practice.

Variety

The utilization of a variety of physical activities provides two benefits. One is physical; the other is psychological. A variety of physical activities, particularly during the early part of the training season, increases the all-around physical development of the athlete and, thereby, improves the peak performance capabilities that may be achieved with rowing specific training.

Basic Training Methodology

The increasing demands of rowing specific training, which necessitates a high volume of training and the utilization of repetitive special exercises, may result in the athlete becoming stale and suffering mental fatigue. Therefore, it is important for the coach to be creative by drawing upon a repertoire of variations in training in order to maintain the athlete's interest and motivation to achieve short and long term performance objectives.

Progressiveness of Training

The improvement of physical performance comes with the adaptation of the human body to a certain quality and quantity of work. After the athlete's body has adapted to the given work, no further improvement can be expected unless an increased training load is used to force the body to a further adoption and, therefore, to a further improvement of physical performance.

Essentially, the training program must provide an adequate amount of work to cause the athlete to become fatigued. After the athlete has had an opportunity to recover and adept, and is thus prepared for an increase in work, the training program must systematically increase the amount of work. This will result in higher levels of adaptation and improved performance capabilities.

Systematization

In the preparation of the training programs, it is necessary to develop a systematic plan. This plan should be based on scientific and training principles and be arranged methodically in a form that organizes the training of the athlete and ensures the proper regularity of training.

The development of a systematic plan will improve the quality of training because the plan would provide a format in which the athlete and coach could test, monitor and control performance capabilities. A systematic plan will also provide a model to be reviewed and revised for the next training season and throughout the athlete's career.

Periodization

Periodization is the process of dividing an annual training program into periods of training to allow the program to be set into manageable segments and to ensure a correct peaking for the main competition or training objective of the year.

The process of periodization depends on the use of the concepts of training loads and the wave principle of training. This information will enable better understanding of the principal components of periodization: training period, training cycle and training session.

Training Load

The training load consists of the quantity and quality of work. Quantity is represented by distance of work, time of work, or number of repetitions, etc. Thus, a rowing training session may be described as, for example, 16 kilometres in distance during which 3 repetitions of 10 minutes of work will be performed. Quality is the effort exerted in the training session. It may be represented as the speed of running, the amount of weight lifted, heart rate maintained, or, in the boat, a combination of pressure applied on the blade and the stroke rating, etc. Thus, the example rowing training session above may be further described as 3 repetitions of 10 minutes of work at a rating of 26 strokes per minute while maintaining a heart rate of 140-170. In a systematic plan of training, the training load goes from quantity to quality. This means that, after a period of adjusting to a new training season, the training starts with a large quantity of a relatively low or medium quality of work to provide all-around development and improvement in endurance capabilities. As the training season progresses, there is a gradual increase in quality and a corresponding decrease in quantity. This enables the development of the specific needs of the sport of rowing and the necessary performance capabilities to achieve the training objective.

Basic Training Methodology

Although this procedure is for the major part of the program, it must be considered as a guide because training in any period of the year is complex and must cover all aspects of the work requirements of rowing.

Training Cycles - The Wave Principle of Training

The training cycle is a limited period of training, usually

between 4 and 8 weeks, during which the programme is directed toward a certain training objective. Training cycles follow the wave principle of applying alternating phases of increasing and decreasing training load.

It has been demonstrated that this step or wave approach is more efficient than the linear or continuous method of loading. As opposed to the continuous method, the wave principle requires that a training load increase must be followed by a decrease in training load during which the athlete's body is able to recover and adapt to the training load. This enables the athlete to be subjected to progressively increasing training loads.

It has also been demonstrated that the best results in improvement of performance can be achieved if the training load is gradually increased during three successive training sessions up to the athlete's maximum load capability for example 50%, 75%, 100%) and followed by a very light training session or a complete rest. This applies to training programs of five or more sessions per week. If the frequency of training sessions is less, the program can be designed with one day off after every outing and with the training load being gradually increased to its maximum on the weekend.

The wave principle of changing the training loads will apply throughout the training cycle, which means that the maximum load will vary from week to week creating the wave approach to training. Appendix A provides an example of this principle.

Planning each Training Period

A systematic training program based on scientific and training principles is fundamental to the successful pursuit of high level athletic performance. The systematic training programme is developed by working in reverse chronological order from the date of the main competition or training objective and dividing the training season into the appropriate number of training periods. Each period has different aims and, to some extent, will continue the application of the concepts of training load and the wave principle of training.

The periodization of the training season may be represented as follows:

A. Preparation Period (six months).

B. Competition Period (five months).

C. Transition Period (one month).

The aims of each period are:

A. Preparation Period.

1. To develop general physical fitness.

2. To develop rowing technique, specific physical fitness for rowing and psychological preparedness for the coming competition period.

B. Competition Period.

1. Further development of rowing technique, specific physical fitness for rowing and psychological preparedness for competition mainly by training in the boat.

2. To develop and stabilize competition performance.

C. Transition Period.

1. Physical and mental relaxation.

2. Relief from the pattern of systematic training.

Planning each Training Cycle

Each period is divided into one or more training cycles of 4 to 8 weeks in length. The plan for each cycle gives the athlete an outline of the particular activities on the land

and in the boat. It shows the kinds of exercises, the quantity and quality of the work, and a detailed program for each training session in the cycle. The plan for each cycle takes into consideration the different degrees of training load and rest intervals within the week and within the whole cycle.

Planning each Training Session

The aim of the period and cycle and the purpose of each session should be carefully explained to the athlete. Every training session must begin with a good warm up on the land 5 to 10 min. of light jogging and 5 min. of mobility exercises) and also in the boat (systems of warm up in the boat vary from crew to crew.

After the warm up in the boat, there is a time for technical exercises because the teaching of technique or correction of technical faults requires mental concentration, which deteriorates with the increasing fatigue of the athlete during the training session. After the technical exercises have been completed, the main part of the session is devoted to the principal aim of the training period and the training cycle. The last part of the training session is for relaxation and a warm down. During the training session, the coach should present a clear purpose for the session by keeping unnecessary communication to a minimum and concentrating on a few important points that will assist the athlete in maintaining the proper focus during each session. At the conclusion of each session, the coach should exchange observations with the athlete or crew and evaluate the session. This procedure will assist in the process of monitoring and controlling the training program and, thereby, increasing the benefits to be derived from each future training session.

A Yearly Training Program

It is important to realize that these programs must be adapted to the specific needs of your athletes giving consideration to their individual state of development and future training objectives.

Planning A Training Programme

An annual training program is the most important tool for the coach to direct and guide athletic training over the training year. It is based on the principles of training and the concept of periodization.

Planning a training program requires a clear understanding of the objective of the program and a procedure to achieve the objective. This purpose may be accomplished by utilizing the following guidelines:

1. Establish an objective.
2. Develop a systematic plan.
3. Implement the plan.
4. Monitor and review the plan.

4.1 Establish an Objective

The objective of a training program will be the achievement of a defined performance level at a designated competition. This competition may occur at the culmination of either a few months of training (a short term objective) or many years of training (a long term objective). It should be noted that, as athletic potential may only be optimised by year round training, emphasis should be placed upon the development of year round training programs.

Develop a Systematic Plan

A systematic plan is developed by working in reverse chronological order from the date of the objective of the plan and dividing the training season into the appropriate number of training periods. This procedure is called periodization (see section 3.0) and may be represented as

demonstrated. It is important to realize that a systematic plan must be developed in conjunction with an understanding of how to implement the plan. This is probably the most difficult aspect of designing and monitoring a training programme. It requires an understanding of the basic principles of training, the concepts of training loads and training cycles , the energy systems, proper rowing technique and the methodology of learning.

Implement the Plan

The coach and athlete must make a conscious decision to proceed with the plan and become active participants in the training process. This ensures that the athlete maintains the proper motivation in the pursuit of the training objective and that the athlete trains regularly and conscientiously.

Monitor and Review the Plan

It is important that the plan includes various tests and standards that are to be attempted and successfully completed, both on and off the water, during the training season. These tests and standards will provide valuable information on the athlete's developing capabilities and on the effectiveness of the plan in directing the athlete towards the training objective.

As well, it is important that both the coach and athlete maintain a training journal to document their observations and comments about the training. This information is invaluable in the process of reviewing the plan both during and after the training season. This review will allow modification to be made in the programme during the season and from season to season to enhance the athlete's opportunity to achieve his or her athletic potential.

This procedure for the planning of a training programme should be repeated for each new training season in order to develop a training programme that is appropriate to the growing and everchanging needs of the athlete.

Summary

The information presented in this course will enable you, the coach, to prepare training programmes that will assist your athletes in the achievement of their training objectives. This ability will be enhanced after practice and years of experience. This "Training Program for Clubs" is based on The FISA Development Club Program distributed in 1993. Many coaches have asked for an update, but in training methodology and rowing technique not much has changed, and the basic stays the same. Anyhow; some training-models has been improved and distribution of time looks a bit different.

The difference from 1993 is the higher number of hours invested in training by the international elite. With more than 40 hours a week in training a lot of injuries in form of stress fractures and lower back problems occurred. Among the lightweight rowers it looks as if the immune defense got strongly reduced and common colds, influenza and other fever-related illnesses caused many breaks in the training system.

This is probably a result of high training load and reduced intake of food to keep the weight down. A problem we must address strongly in the time to come. In this program we have two new appendixes presenting a better program for flexibility and series of additional exercises to give the clubs the possibility to create a more "all-round" training program and avoid "disharmony" between the different groups of muscles. Many injuries could be related to underdevelopment in non-specific rowing muscles.

15

Measuring on Soft Skills Training - An Approach Document

The biggest problem with the ROI claim is the let ter I , which stands for Investment. Cont rary to almost all thinking in this profession, t raining is not an investment - it is simply an expense. While " investment " sounds more important than expense, t raining is nonetheless, an expense. " I nvestment " is a business term that implies the adding of capital to an organizat ion. Unfortunately, "human capital does not qualify. Unt il a t raining vendor will sell a course to you, and then buy it back for more than you paid, you did not invest in t raining, you spent money on t raining. Peter Drucker was right when he said, Market ing and innovat ion make money. Everything else is a cost .

Not yet convinced it 's worth the money to spend on an expensive consultant or t raining seminar? Read on True, it may take some t ime to see return on investment . However, in almost all cases, soft skills' training is well worth the t ime and money in the long run. As Nierenberg points out , the results may not be immediate but improving interact ion and people skills leads to bet ter assignments down the road. Your most important element is your human capital," she says. Unless you have the soft skills, you can't get to the hard skills. Company management wants to know that the money they are spending on t raining is well spent . They want to know that they are get t ing a sufficient return on their t raining/investment. Improvement factors include increased product ivity, reduct ion of waste, and improved employee retention. Measurement of t raining ROI starts with defining the reasons and goals for the t raining, determining how much the t raining will cost, and verifying the amount of return.

Quest ions you may have to include before you spend on training:

What is the reason for the training

What is the investment in training

How is the return measured

Start with training goals

A company may provide t raining to their workers, managers, customers, and somet imes suppliers. The ult imate reason for t raining them should be to improve the profits and repeat business of the company. It is preferred that this improvement is measurable, so that an effect ive ROI can be determined. If there are no well defined "measurable goals" then don't even start the t raining process.

Reasons to train workers

The reason to train workers and managers is so they will learn to do their jobs bet ter or perhaps learn new skills or technologies that can be applied to the company's goals. Somet imes workers and managers are t rained to sat isfy government requirements, to ensure safety, or to prevent lawsuits or other forms of company loss. Managers are often trained in people-handling skills. Also, companies may allow workers to take t raining simply as a way to keep them happy in their jobs.

Investment in training

I n order to train personnel a company must pay for the development of t raining material and the t ime spent by the t rainers in the classroom. This is either absorbed through an in-house t raining department , paid to outside t raining companies, or a combinat ion of the two. Costs include paying for t ime off from work, paying t rainers, and t ravel and lodging expenses.

Time spent by w orkers

Workers and managers must often take t ime off from work to at tend training classes. Not only is the company paying wages for no work done, but it may also lose opportunit ies for more sales or product ivity during the absence of the personnel. For off-site t raining, the company may also have to pay for t ravel and lodging. The burdened hourly rate, est imated loss of product ivity, and t raining expenses must be calculated.

Keep t rack of costs

Obviously, if a company wants to determine their ROI for t raining, they must account for all the money spent , especially the hidden expenses.

Measuring the ROI

The greatest factor in measuring the return-on-investment for t raining is the definition of what the t raining is to achieve. Measuring the amount of money generated by a group before and after the t raining, and then comparing that improvement with the cost of the t raining is the way to measure the ROI .

If no measurable goals

Very often there are no specific or measurable goals to

achieve for a training session. This is especially t rue in many of the "soft skills" taught to managers. I t is very difficult to measure the results of a manager style t raining seminar. I n fact , the goal for such training might be something like. To be a bet ter manager," whatever that means. I f there is no way to measure the effect iveness of the training, the company might be bet ter off simply giving the people money to go on a vacat ion.

Having specific goals or Key Per formance I ndicators

I f the goal is to improve the product ivity of a worker in a certain process, a met ric must be determined that leads to a company bot tom line number. Before and after t raining measurements must be made to determine the effect iveness of the t raining sessions. Then the costs involved in t raining the personnel can be compared with the real improvement of profits to determine its ROI .

For example, safety t raining has a specific goal of reducing the accident rate. Stat ist ics can be made that will verify the effect iveness of such t raining. The reason to t rain should be to improve the company's bot tom line. The investment in t raining consists of the cost of the training and the t ime spent by the personnel from their jobs. By measuring the effect on the company profits before and after t raining, and then comparing with the costs of the t raining, a company can determine their returnon-investment .

Key per formance indicators

So the best place to start is ident ifying key performance indicators (KPI s) . But then what? "Start ing with the KPI , ident ify the key act ivit ies that have to happen for successful achievement of the measure and for each act ivity, ident ify the competency requirements, especially those with most leverage over the outcome," says Tony Dunk, principal of HR consultancy CDA's t raining and development business. For example, the KPI might be a customer retent ion measure, where one cont ribut ing act ivity is to reduce customer losses by dealing with complaints effect ively, so a key soft skill is dealing with angry customers. I n this case, Dunk says that we can measure the customer losses both before and after the 'dealing with angry customers' training, quant ify the improvement , and set it against the cost of the training.

"Where it is difficult is to take a generic t raining Programme on handling difficult customers, and answer the quest ion 'what is the ROI for the Programme' when it isn't within the context of a specific KPI ," says Dunk.

"This is why t raining departments often find it difficult to establish ROI for their curricula, because their needs analysis often drives generic development across the organisat ion, without a real understanding of the financial need being addressed in specific areas of the business.

That and the fact that they only tend to do it when the budget comes under scrut iny."

Hence one needs to keep in mind that ROI on generic programs is not really measurable.

Donald Taylor is st rategic alliances director at management software company I nfoBasis and chairman of the Learning Technologies conference. He says that when calculat ing the ROI on any t raining, results need to focus on core areas such as product ivity, morale and staff turnover, which are in line with business needs and are of clear value to the organisat ion.

" It 's crucial that alignment to business needs is done up front with t raining, so that when you are asked ret rospect ively whether there has been value added, you have clear answers," he says.

Skills audit

According to Taylor, this means ensuring that t raining is aligned to an ongoing skills audit . " I f you are on top of which skills each role requires and because roles are defined by business needs, it can illust rate how t raining bridges that gap," he says.

Declan Mulkeen, market ing director at communicat ion and cultural awareness t raining provider Communicaid, agrees that for soft skills t raining it is vital to understand that effect ive programmes will have an impact on end behaviour.

Once it is clear what changes in behaviour you require and you have determined their potent ial impact on business performance, it is possible to t ranslate them into tangible met rics, which can be measured financially," he says.

Mulkeen cites the example of measuring the ROI on cultural awareness t raining given to employees before being sent on an internat ional assignment . "Assignments are very expensive for any organisat ion, with costs typically four to five t imes' the annual salary of the employee. By providing pre-assignment t raining, you can reduce the failure rate. As you understand what you want to measure and possess a clear vision of the outcomes you require, it is then possible to establish ROI , he says.

However, Mulkeen does have a word of warning: on its own ROI cannot determine whether t raining has been t ruly successful. "Don't forget delegate feedback, line manager and team 360-degree reviews as well as pre- and post - t raining assessments and examinat ions. Other measures of t raining should always be considered to evaluate whether it was a successful init iat ive," he adds.

Top tips

1) Before measuring ROI , make sure the t raining solut

ion is aligned with core business needs

2) Use an ongoing skills audit to provide evidence of why t raining in specific areas is needed

3) Be clear on object ives and ident ify key performance indicators (KPI s) to measure t raining against

4) Est imate outcomes from the start - do not start t raining Programme unless the init ial expectat ion of benefits improvement is just ified by the cost .

The benefits that w ould be felt anyw ay w hether you do ROI calculat ion or not :

Whilst qualitat ive results are hard to quantify, we believe there are many tangible benefits to invest ing a lit t le more t ime to ensure that soft -skills t raining is as effect ive as it can be. These include creating enabling:

a) **Dynamic w orking culture** - Team members become bet ter equipped to problem solve posit ively and proact ively, and they have the determinat ion to st rive for excellence.

b) **Successful implementat ion of change** - Effect ive leadership, individual mot ivat ion and improved communicat ion brings act ive involvement , and commitment to planned changes.

c) **Increased sat isfact ion** - Improved communicat ion and an open, dynamic working culture improves overall sat isfact ion and commitment .

d) **Reduct ion in staff turnover** - A more sat isfied and commit ted, less st ressed workforce is less likely to move on. Salary and other benefits become less important when team members feel respected appreciated and supported.

e) **More efficient meet ings** - Open and honest

communicat ion and effect ive facilitat ion of meet ings saves t ime and improves collaborat ive problem solving and decision-making.

f) **Meeting of deadlines** – More effect ive communicat ion and negot iat ion between departments means that targets are more likely to be met because of increased t ransparency, t rust and rapport .

g) **Increased product ivity** – Through effect ive leadership, improved mot ivat ion and communicat ion, individuals and teams are bet ter equipped to achieve results.

h) **Saving of managerial time** - Improved team communicat ion and collaborat ive problem solving results in fewer conflicts and fewer demands on management t ime.

i) **Reduction in complaints** – Improved collaborat ion, negot iat ion and resolut ion of problems results in fewer grievances, and a reduct ion in internal and external complaints.

In summary, 'Soft Skills' Training can and does offer ROI through sustainable and valuable improvements, part icular ly when:

1) It is st rategically linked to individual, team and organisat ional needs

2) It addresses individual, team and organisat ional at t itudes to change

3) It is supported by on-going reinforcements by managers and team members

4) It is followed by real opportunit ies to pract ice "how to"

Training In Sustainable Development

Dr. Manibhai Desai Management Training Centre at Warje in Pune aims at transfer of technologies and replication of our successful programmes on a wider scale. Apart from tailormade short duration training modules, demonstrations are also organised at BAIF campuses at Urulikanchan (Maharashtra), Lakkihalli (Karnataka), Vansda, Nanodra and Krishi Vigyan Kendra, Chaswad (Gujarat). Several documentary films and books have been brought out to promote various technologies on natural resource management and environmental protection. BAIF is publishing a House Journal and Newsletter to share its field experiences with other organizations.

BAIF believes Management is a critical factor for smooth implementation of development programmes. In the absence of any background in Management, the community workers, extension officers and field guides working with BAIF, implement the programmes based on their experience and guidance from development specialists within the organisation. Moreover, there is no formal institution in the country for imparting training in sound management of development programmes for such cadres.

Realsing the fact that capacity building of Development Managers working in the field is the key to organisational development, BAIF set up the Dr. Manibhai Desai Management Training Centre (MDMTC) in 1993 at Warje, Pune. The Indian Institute of Management - Ahmedabad contributed to the initial institution building, faculty development, research and documentation efforts, while the International Agricultural Centre in The Netherlands provided guidance for course development.

Objectives

The MDMTC imparts training with the following objectives in mind

* Capacity building and skills development of the community based on management approaches and skills
* Sharing of experiences
* Transfer of technologies and replication of successful programmes on a wider scale

Faculty

Training is imparted by BAIF's multi-disciplinary team of experts who are directly involved in programme implementation and have vast experience in grassroots development. In order to maintain a balance between field experiences and theoretical principles, the faculty comprises of the core training team, selected BAIF Programme Managers, and associated Visiting Faculty.

The core team, drawn from senior techno-managerial staff at BAIF, is responsible for the design, planning, execution and periodic review of training and related activities.

Target Group and Areas of Training

MDMTC offers tailor-made management development programmes for the benefit of its field workers as well as outside agencies such as Government Organisations, Civil Society Organisations, progressive leaders of Panchayati Raj Institutions and Corporate Organisations in the following areas:

* Livestock Development
* Horticulture Development
* Improved Agriculture
* Agricultural Economics
* Watershed Development and Management

* Social Sciences
* Project Management

To ensure hands-on experience, field demonstrations and exposure visits are also arranged to various project locations of BAIF. Apart from tailor-made short duration training modules, demonstrations are also organised at BAIF campuses at Urulikanchan Maharashtra, Lakkihalli (Karnataka), Vansda, Nanodra and Krishi Vigyan Kendra, Chaswad Gujarat. Several documentary films and books have been brought out to promote various technologies on natural resource management and environmental protection. BAIF is publishing various Journals and Newsletter to share its field experiences with other organisations.

Facilities

Located on National Highway No 4., Mumbai-Bangalore Byepass Road, the MDMTC campus offers the following facilities

* Four Training Classrooms each with a sitting capacity of 30 participants
* Conference Room (AC) to accommodate 25 participants
* Seminar hall with a sitting capacity of 200 persons
* A well furnished Guest House to accommodate 60 persons
* A spacious dining hall offering vegetarian cuisine and meal-plans covering bed tea/coffee, breakfast, lunch, in-session tea/coffee and dinner
* Information Resource Centre with a rich collection of books, journals and CD databases

* Communication facilities including internet and E-mail access
* Indoor and outdoor recreation facilities

Proposed Training Programmes

MDMTC plans to provide training in the following fields

* Management development programmes for the middle mangement cadre of BAIF
* Technical skill programmes for non-technical staff
* Capacity development programmes for representatives of People's organisations established by BAIF for sustainability of the programme.

Approach to Training Extension Personel

One of the important mandate of the KVK is to organize training programmes for inservice grass root level extension personnel. In this section therefore, approach to training of extension personnel has been dealt briefly.

There are mainly three models of training. These are: i) discrete phases or traditional model, ii) interdependent and interrelated process model; and iii) system model.

The Discrete Phases Model is most frequently used training model consists of five discrete phases connected sequentially; assessment, objective setting, design, implementation and evaluation. Each phase stands independently of the other phases. It has several consequences; i) needs assessment data are prematurely organized and stated as training needs which results in; ii) objectives stated in very general and unmeasurable terms and not closely related to the real training needs which leads to; iii) programmes designed and implemented which are only slightly related to the real training needs or "real life" circumstances faced by trainees. In general, this model of training leads to increasingly more general and less precise training efforts.

The Interdependent and Interrelated Process Model is used in which the five phases form sub processes which are highly interrelated and interdependent on all other subprocesses as well as on the total process.

The Systems Model is a problem-solving process that places the diagnosis of needs before the presentation of methods required to achieve the needs. It is a discipline that requires those responsible for designing and providing the training that people need to carry out a series of interdependent steps in a logical sequence. The details of this model follow as it is suited to KVK in-service training. The System Model consists of a number of subsystems which are interdependent.

The System model is a diagnostic approach. It diagnoses the performance problem. It prescribes remedy only after a careful diagnosis of the problem. It develops the training systems in five distinct and sequential phases of development. For developing a training system model, each phase is described here briefly.

Phase 1: Training Needs Assessment

This phase starts by first posing the basic question: What is the performance problem? If the answer is the gap between the desirable and the actual job performance by extension personnel, it asks the next question; what is this gap which is required to be overcome by training? In other word, what are the training needs of extension personnel? The training needs are assessed as objectively as possible, drawing a clear distinction between 'actual' and 'imagined' needs of extension personnel.

Training needs should be assessed at three levels namely,

- Individual
- Groups
- Organizational.

A number of methods for training needs assessment are available for different levels. The training needs have to be assessed within the ambit of national priorities and programmes and farmers' felt needs for training. It is essential to realize that farmers' felt needs for training lay the foundation upon which the training needs of extension personnel are required to be assessed.

Phase II: Training Plans Development

After assessment of training needs appropriate training plans are required to be developed on the basis of assessed training needs of extension personnel. A training plans can be (a) short-term, (b) long term, or both. While an Annual Training Plan is an essential requirement of sound training arrangement it is desirable that training plans are develop in, say, a five year framework. The advantage of developing training plans in a 5 year framework is that management will have a reduced task of undertaking an annual review only, enabling it to devote more time to other aspects of training management, which will enhance the value of training.

Phase III: Design of Training Programmes:

In the third phase, appropriate training programmes are required to be designed after training needs assessment (Phase I) and in accordance with the developed training plans (Phase II). The starting point in the design of the training programme is a statement of its objectives. The objectives should be stated clearly and in simple, straightforward language. The use of jargon should be avoided. The objectives, not more than 3 or 5 in number, should clearly state the Knowledge, Skills, and Attitudes the trainee will acquired after the training and how will it be useful to the trainee in his job performance. The statement of objectives should enable the trainee to have a clear idea about the relevance of training programme to his training needs.

The next step is the determination of an appropriate mix of various skills required by extension personnel. Broadly, extension personnel require three types of skills, namely, i) technical, ii) human and iii) conceptual. The mix of these skills will be different for different levels of extension personnel. Weights can be attached to different skills for determination of mix. For example, the mix for Village Extension Workers can be upto 50 percent technical skills, 40 percent human skills and 10 per cent conceptual skills.

Appropriate curriculum then can be developed by following the Concentric Circles Approach to Curriculum. Under this approach there are three concentric circles, the inner circle of what must be known, the middle circle of what should be known, and the outer circle of what could be known. It is imperative that the curriculum concentrates upon the inner circle of what must be known and does not drift to the outer circle of what could be known, as it very often happens in practice.

The selection of an appropriate training methods is the next step in the design of a training programme. An array training methods are available suited to different levels of extension personnel. As a general rule, a mix of training methods is preferable to only one training method, and the entire programme must have a problem-solving practical orientation.

Practical assignments and providing adequate opportunities to trainees for interaction will enhance the utility of and receptivity of training.

Training technology now offers a number of training

aids which can increase and reinforce learning. These include a number of visual aids like chalkboard, flip chart, plastic writing board, magnetic board, flannel board and overhead projector, and projected aids (like slides, film strips, slide projectors, and video tapes). In addition to audio-visual aids, computers are also emerging as a powerful training aid. Suffice it to say that a variety of training aids are required to be used in a training programme which will sustain the interest of trainees in message receptivity.

With a view to make training an enduring exercise, supporting training material is also required to be developed simultaneously with a training programme or separately as a training input. In the former category fall lecture notes, supporting leaflets and bulletins, and as it usually the case, a compilation of course material. In the latter category fall specially developed training manuals and handbooks which can either be used in a training course or used separately by trainees on their own.

Phase IV: Training Programme Implementation

In the fourth phase, the training programmes are implemented. The implementation of training programmes is the responsibility of KVK, or more precisely, the Course Instructor. Many training programmes flounder due to poor implementation which usually reflects lack of or inadequate preparation. Use of checklist and alertness to respond to an emergency like non appearance of resource person in time can prevent occurrence of many avoidable mishaps. A wise word of counsel is not to take anything for granted and to personally ensure that things are in order.

Phase V: Training Monitoring and Evaluation

In this last phase, training is monitored and evaluated. Training monitoring is relatively greater practical importance than training evaluation. Training monitoring should take place through well developed training monitoring indices like number of training courses planned and held every month and number of trainees planned and covered. The training monitoring indices will differ from level to level. These indices should be regularly brought to the notice of top management so that it can intervene to correct a situation. An evaluation of training by trainers and trainees followed by an annual review by the top management can considerably enhance the usefulness of training courses. Suitable changes in the training approach can be made as and when necessary, on the results of training monitoring and evaluation. Evaluation should be done by the course instructor with a questionnaire having question items related to the coverage of the content methodology of training, audio-visual aids quality, stay arrangement, and communication eliciting responses from the trainees at the end of the training session course. Such responses should be analyzed for making further improvement.

16

Coalition on Women and Job Training

The Coalition on Women and Job Training is committed to ensuring welfare reform is a success for all families. Our advocacy agenda for reauthorization includes promoting a portfolio of supports that will help low income women with children to enter or remain in the workforce. Further, we are committed to promoting the well-being of families who face the most severe barriers to work by ensuring they are provided the services and flexibility that will allow them to become self-sufficient. Families must have the appropriate level of program support and flexibility that will allow them to benefit from the opportunities that TANF provides. The Coalition supports retaining the basic structure of the original bill s emphasis on work and a fiveyear lifetime limit. However, while the current TANF system has focused on caseload reduction, reauthorization must focus on reducing the poverty rates of recipient families.

Education and Job Training

To achieve economic self-sufficiency and adequately provide for their families, TANF participants need jobs that pay a living wage (measured by each state s own self-sufficiency standard), and provide benefits and opportunities for advancement. The law s focus is on a workfirst job placement strategy that places participants in low-wage, low-skilled jobs with limited opportunity for advancement. Employment in high-wage, high-skilled occupations requires access to education and job training for TANF participants.

Allowable Activities

Current law permits states to conduct and administer community service or work experience programs to move recipients into unsubsidized employment.

'£ The coalition believes reauthorization should require states to actively promote education and training activities, including post secondary education

The coalition believes reauthorization should require states to emphasize education and job training that leads to living wage occupations with opportunities for career advancement, including nontraditional employment for women, which is an effective way to raise the earnings of low-income women

Current TANF regulations limit the ability of TANF participants to access education and job training due to restrictive allowable work activities, work participation rates and time limits. In addition, participants may also encounter multiple barriers to educational success and job stability such as limited English proficiency, illiteracy, low educational attainment, or learning disabilities that require additional support services.

Current law limits work activities to include unsubsidized or subsidized employment; workfare; and certain educational activities, such as vocational education (maximum 12 months), education directly related to employment (only applies to high school and teen parents), and secondary school attendance (adult basic education towards a GED, or completion of high school). In addition, there is a 30% cap on the number of persons in all TANF families that a state can allow to participate in any of these educational activities toward fulfillment of their work participation rate. The coalition believes that reauthorization should expand the definition of allowable work activities to include:

Participation in an education program leading to the completion of secondary education, GED or equivalent .Participation in an education program leading to a certificate, associates degree or baccalaureate degree at a post secondary institution. Participation in vocational, career technical education or job training, and " Participation in mental health, domestic violence, or substance abuse treatment and counseling. The coalition believes that reauthorization should eliminate the time limit for participation in the above allowable work activities, and should set realistic time limits for participation in work activities that are adequate for degree or certification completion.

The coalition believes that reauthorization should eliminate caps on the amount of TANF participants states can enroll in allowable work activities The coalition believes that reauthorization must □stop the clock for all TANF participants who are engaged in allowable work activities full-time

Employment Readiness and Retention

Many current and former welfare recipients who have entered the workforce continue to receive poverty level wages. In order to continue to be successful, retain employment and ensure a better quality of life for their children, they will need access to on-going work supports such as child care, job training, transportation, and emergency assistance.

The Coalition recognizes that many families impacted by welfare reform have considerable impediments to entering and sustaining employment. Studies reviewed by the General Accounting Office have documented the high prevalence of domestic violence, substance addiction, mental health and other family hardships among those remaining on welfare caseloads.

In addition to these more recognized barriers, many individuals transitioning into employment from welfare face traditional work and family obstacles such as juggling work and care for sick family members and arranging emergency child care when a child becomes ill. Many of those who have exited welfare programs and remain outside the workforce have similar challenges to entering and sustaining employment. The coalition believes reauthorization should adjust federal work participation requirements to accommodate individuals facing multiple barriers in becoming job-ready, such as. Allowing TANF participants the option of using participation in mental health, domestic violence, or substance abuse treatment and counseling as an allowable work activity

Specifying that TANF participants with certain barriers (such as domestic violence and families with mental health problems and disabled members) are exempt from requirements and not counted in the states performance rates " Increasing the limitation on states exemptions, and "Allowing TANF participants to use the time spent receiving comprehensive services, including life skills development, and the referral and provisions for support services, such as child care and transportation to count toward fulfillment of work requirements.

The C oalition on Women and Job Training is comprised of more than 30 members from national womens, civil rights, religious, and labor organizations. Since its inception in 1992, the Coalition has been at the forefront of the federal debate on job training reform and has worked to increase low-income womens options for achieving economic self-sufficiency through an improved job training system.

17

Training and Development-Its's Role in Achieving Organisation

What happens if we don't and they stay?

Is investment in the area of training and development linked to the bottom line within the business? Increasingly, high performing organisations today are recognising the need to use best training and development practices to enhance their competitive advantage. Training and development is an essential element of every business if the value and potential of it's people is to be harnessed and grown. Many studies have highlighted the clear links between well designed and strategic training and development initiatives and the bottom line within the business. The image of an industry and of individual employers is also influenced by the extent and quality of staff training and development. Potential employees in such an open labour market will assess the track record of prospective employers in this vital area. Career progression and development is an increasingly attractive or even basic requirement for many such employees. In today's business climate where all industries are experiencing staff and skills shortages, companies are faced with stiff internal and external competition for quality employees. Each employer who invests seriously in the area of Training and Development will reap the benefits of an enriched working environment with higher levels of staff retention as well as increased productivity and performance.

In a recent IBEC survey (HR Benchmarking Report 2004), respondents were asked to identify the key drivers of training initiatives over the past year and for the 12 month period ahead. The top three were health and safety, technical changes and customer service. In other words, organisations are now using training and development as an incentive to retain and motivate their people and to be recognised as an employer of choice as well as giving staff the skills and knowledge needed to keep up with technological change and customer service. A further key finding in this survey was that the vast majority of companies surveyed stated they provided support to employees to pursue outside educational programmes. This support consisted of both financial aid as well as time off for both study and exam leave. Both of these initiatives may have benefits which are difficult to quantify, but areas such as staff turnover and morale are clear indicators of success in this field.

While research indicates an increased interest in and awareness of the benefits of training, the question needs to be asked as to whether this translated into Irish organisations establishing training policies and or increasing their spend on training.

A National Survey of Training and Development in Ireland conducted by Garavan and Heraty in 2003 outlined a number of key trends which are emerging in the Training arena in Ireland. Some of the key ones include the following:

Irish organisations spend on average 3.55% of payroll on training which does not compare favourably with other EU member states. (The IBEC HR Benchmarking Survey indicates a figure of 3.15%).

The average number of days training provided per

employee per year in 2004 was 5.35. (IBEC HR Benchmarking Survey indicates an average figure of 3-5 days).

There is evidence of a positive attitude to training and development among those surveyed with many viewing it to be an important component in the organisation's strategy.

Smaller firms are more likely to deliver training in an ad hoc way with larger companies applying a more formal approach to managing training.

Line managers and employees seem to have a greater role in the organisation and design of training and development. There is still a strong usage of the traditional forms of learning strategies including classroom teaching and subject driven courses, although there is a growth in the use of new technology to deliver training.

Learning in teams is an increasingly popular form of learning in the workplace. Employees are now taking more personal ownership for their own development.

However, the percentage spend and number of days spent training staff may be useful in order to get an overview of the companies commitment to training and development, but it is the manner, approach and content of the training initiatives as well as their assessment and follow up which determine success. It is all too easy to throw money at a performance problem and assume that a training course will sort it out, when this may well be just putting a plaster over an open wound. Training initiatives need to be strategically aligned to the overall company mission and goals. They need to be designed and delivered with the aim of helping staff to achieve their departmental as well as personal goals, so the trend of increased involvement by line managers and employees is a positive development in terms of ownership of the training and learning. By adopting a strategic approach to training and development rather than an unplanned and ad hoc one, training and development initiatives become more targeted, measurable and effective. However, increased flexibility in terms of training delivery may need to be expanded in the future to facilitate participant's different learning styles as well as lifestyles. They also need to be assessed in terms of reaction, learning, behaviour change and results to determine the added value to the organisation. This area of evaluation is one whereby many organisations simply evaluate the effectiveness of the training intervention based on the initial reaction of participants, an area which clearly needs to be expanded. A sample training and development approach is outlined below describing the essential elements in a strategic approach.

In order to remain competitive and to ensure excellent staff are attracted to and remain within the organisation, companies need to ensure that the training and development of all employees is an issue which is taken seriously. By investing in the development of the people who are the face of the business, companies can get ahead of the competition and excel in what they do. One of the most important aspects of managing people lies in helping employees become more effective at their jobs and being able to adapt to that job or another job as he/she matures within the organisation. This requires a high level of co-ordination between employee training and development and the range of other personnel functions, such as recruitment and selection, performance appraisal, reward systems and employee relations.

Identification of a company's training needs, designing a relevant training plan, selecting and implementing the resulting training programme and evaluating it's success are therefore integral elements of the overall Human Resource process. However, for any of these functions to be effective, the Training plans and policies must be in line with the organisation's strategic objectives. The Training function is increasingly considered to be a key player in helping the organisation to achieve it's goals through it's people as it is becoming more generally accepted that there is a strong correlation between organisational success and investment in training and development. There is now a growing awareness of the importance of a planned approach to training and development as a tool for competitive advantage, staff recruitment, selection, retention and motivation.

The whole Training and Development function has increasingly acquired status as the instrument for breaking new ground and bringing about change through its developmental activities. Training managers must provide expert advice to top level management, usually about the value to the organisation of a particular kind of training. Furthermore, they must have the means to persuade management as to a systematic approach to training outlining for example, the extent to which changes in structure and procedures will be necessary to support training. The training must take place within a framework of partnership between the trainer, employer and employee.

This relationship must be characterised by trust between all stakeholders so that training does not simply reflect the views of the employer. This commonality of interest must be identified and worked towards. Training and development is about making a difference to the bottom line, both in terms of how people feel about their jobs as well as in the area of performance and productivity. Ultimately, it is about adding real value to the organisation and those who comprise it.

18

Method for Rapid Development of Training Materials

This paper describes the literature search effort instituted by small group of university academic and staff personnel assigned to assume software training responsibilities for 2,400 university faculty and 1,200 staff and the resulting training materials products and processes developed internally based on the literature search to meet these needs. The result of the effort has been extremely successful and is fully documented, described and illustrated.

The training material content, aimed at identifying learner outcomes in terms of work product completion rather than software feature exposure, and the rapid method for design and development of training materials lends itself to productive collaboration and work-sharing among training staff and a high degree of consistency of result. Further research explorations focused on this method and its products are identified.

Introduction

The replacement of a software system with an upgraded version, the installation of new software into a working environment, and the training of instructors and students to use software they have not previously used has become such a common process that it can readily be viewed as a fact of modern life. Two cases suffice to illustrate this point. Tens of millions of computer users are finding it necessary to "re-learn" much of what they know of personal productivity software by the changes imposed by Microsoft's massive redesign of its office suite from prior versions to Office 2007. The new software version, released in November 2006, was downloaded by 3.5 million users for the beta test (Microsoft, 2006) and the changes affect tens of millions of people. In another area, instructors are finding it necessary to learn significantly new software operations as they move from earlier versions of Blackboard's Course Learning Management System (C, LMS) to it version 8 which has radically changed grading and discussion board components (Blackboard, 2008). Since Blackboard commands the major share of C, LMS installations, numbering well over 3,000, this change affects 300,000 to perhaps one million instructors.

Instructional Technology Development, a unit of DePaul University's Information Services Division, was given the responsibility in 2006 to consolidate a unit of trainers and technical support personnel to accomplish software upgrade training for 3,600 employees, comprising 2,400 faculty and 1,200 administrative staff. In order to accomplish this as effectively as possible the unit was formed with experienced trainers as well as faculty actively engaged in classroom and distance learning teaching. In order to inform this effort a focused literature review on training materials development was initiated with the goal of optimizing training materials development for the intended audience. One result of this effort, which is now an ongoing involvement with research in the area of adult learning, was the development of a format and a method for software training materials that has proven especially suitable, effective, and flexible, which is rapid to implement and has been well received. This brief paper describes some of the results of our literature search, the training materials format we developed based on it, the method we evolved to develop these materials, and suggestions for possible further research.

Characteristics of Effective Learning Materials for Adults

Adult learning and development researchers tell us that adults prefer instruction that is self-directed, reflexive, experiential, relevant, solution-oriented, and transformative learner's biases and assumptions are challenged. Training must also activate, affirm and build upon prior knowledge and real-world experience and have immediate and practical application.

This sums up perhaps better than any other single statement the essence of effective professional development training.

Our review of the relevant literature, however, identified the work of several others that also has a direct bearing on the way in which software training materials can be developed for maximum learner benefit. Bannert explored the utility of minimizing the software feature set to which learners were initially exposed and also compared the effectiveness of instructor-led materials with self-instruction materials, and determined that in his experiments user satisfaction and acceptance of the various training approaches was identical, yet learners experiencing self-learning materials "achieved significantly better learning outcomes than students in the 'human tutor' group. Bannert also found that while learners exposed to a subset of system functionality learned significantly faster, they did not in contrast to the assumptions of Carroll, upon whose "training wheels" approach his work rested experience better learning outcomes. Leutner identified that focusing on a subset of software functionality first, and gradually expanding the focus, while at the same time beginning with heavy guidance and gradually relaxing it, were more effective as a strategy than any other combination and manipulation of these factors, and confirmed that ignoring these factors in the design of a training approach for software almost invariably was less effective. Venkatesh and David determined that prior to handson experience with a new software system, a user's perception of the ease of use of the system is based primarily on the individual's own self-conception of their computer skills in general, but that an objective sense of system usability is gained after direct experience. Further, the nature of that sense of usability is tied intimately to the nature of the direct experience and the satisfaction, or lack of satisfaction, experienced by the person in that contact.

(Venkatesh and Davis, 1996). Yi and Davis accomplished an in-depth validation of and evolution of an observational learning model confirming that training in which a learner observes how a task is accomplished and then models the same behavior produces superior training outcomes to those of approaches relying more heavily on the theory behind an operation or recitation of the results of an action. Ricci et al. studied whether an approach to training in which new skills are taught as part of a game were as or more effective than traditional step-by-step explanation and drill and determined that the game approach was superior in specific instances. Especially insightful is very explicit human-computer interface analysis of training materials provided by Carroll, Smith-Kerker, Ford, and Mazur-Rimetz in describing the design and formation of a "minimal manual" guide for the development of self-instruction materials, which combines the development of very specific notions of instructional material content and expression with focused experiments to evaluate the outcome of their use. With the exception of the work of Ricci et. al. the approach we settled on for the development of training materials for the university environment relied on and benefited from all of the findings of this prior research. Rather than trying to invent a new wheel from scratch, we very much felt that our efforts benefited from the knowledge already gained by others in this area.

Defining Requirements

The primary intent of the training materials development process undertaken was the provision of materials that could serve the purpose of instructor-led training to be conducted in one to three hour sessions. However it was also necessary to envision that the same materials should be useful to learners for self-instruction and reference purposes. It was anticipated that training sessions would be conducted in a lab setting accommodating as many as personnel at a session with each participant seated at a live computer capable of accessing the software which was the object of the training. It was projected that the incoming skill level of participants would vary considerably even for training which was segregated by content as to a new user or existing user audience. Further, a time constraint existed at the outset to provide initial learning materials for the most critical training needs within a relatively short timeframe, with additional materials to follow within a period of weeks thereafter. The specific content of training materials on the immediate agenda included Blackboard for faculty (both new users and users familiar with simple processes), Endnote, a locally-developed survey tool named QuickData, audio presentation preparation, editing and podcast provision, video presentation preparation, editing and presentation, and the impending university-wide upgrade of the Microsoft Office Suite from 2003 to 2007. All of this was to be accomplished with a staff of two training materials developers and three trainers, with considerable overlap between these two sets of personnel, housed organizationally in an area also populated with technical support personnel, audio visual technicians and the team of Blackboard administrators.

Implementation of the Training Materials Design

The principles and beneficial practices derived from our literature search led directly to the design goals to be met by an optimal (or, at the least, a superior) type of learning materials. The materials had to:

- be concise—contain the minimum necessary verbiage to accomplish the purpose
- provide focused coverage of specific topics with work-related outcomes relevant to the audience
- provide coverage in context to incur the minimum necessary learner orientation to applicability
- be intuitive in nature and require no, or an absolute minimum, of additional explanation
- lend themselves to accurate, consistent, and rapid learner interpretation.

By fortuitous circumstance it became evident that it is possible to satisfy many of these requirements with an implementation method that not only provides the desired product but also is substantially faster to implement than the traditional "user manual" approach stemming from the legacy of early technical writing. The user manual approach begins with the assumption that written materials are primarily that: words supported by focused illustrations. The approach we developed to meet the design goals reverses this and recognizes that when software training is the goal the object of focus is the entire screen viewed by the user. Words are secondary and their placement must reflect the primacy of this fact and the overwhelming importance of the context provided by the entire screens viewed by the user, which literally is the software system to the user. The image can be resized to fit the slide by grabbing a corner and moving it diagonally toward the center, then aligning a corner of the image to the corner of the slide and sizing it to completely fill the slide. In the case of webbased software accessed via a browser, the "crop" function of Powerpoint 2007 can be used to trim out the top part of the screen and the status line at the bottom to reduce visual clutter and provide room for a concise instructional message area at the top of the slide. (Alternatively, the screen image can be pasted into a photo editor and the cropping action done with the editor, and the image output as file to be inserted into a slide. This method has the advantage of actually reducing the size of the graphic image, while the internal crop function leaves the image at its original storage space requirement. In addition to the top of screen instructional verbiage,

stand-out block arrows, heavy circle borders, or inset text boxes in a distinctive color can be used on the screen image itself to call attention to items. The intention with these is to provide the kind of attention-drawing visualization analogous to that which would occur if an instructor were standing next to the learner, looking over his or her shoulder, and physically pointing out the item and identifying and explaining important points about it. The intention of using full-screen images in all cases is to avoid the kind of "out of context" learner confusion that often ensues when only a fragment of a screen is illustrated, which is almost always the case if training materials are viewed as traditional "user manuals" or ordinary technical writing.

Results and Outcome

Implementation of the chosen design has proceeded smoothly and we have found that the following method for development of a new set of training materials has provided consistently superior results:

1. Inventory the basic functions of interest to learners at a given pre-training course level. This is done by interviewing a key set of end users prior to training materials development, examining the functionality of the software being replaced or upgraded, and by relying on the experience of faculty members who serve on the Instructional Technology Development staff.

2. Identify the end products or things learners will know how to produce or accomplish by taking the training—the specific work products they will be enabled to create, not the steps or software functions to which they will be exposed.

3. Sequence the topics to be covered within a training course and develop a hands-on exercise for each. Break a complete exercise into steps that can be expressed in a few lines.

4. Perform the step-by-step sequence of operations needed to accomplish each exercise and capture each screen, creating a slide in the pattern illustrated in Figure 1. Explanatory words (if needed) are carefully chosen and edited so that they are concise and not verbose, so that they always fit within the top border area and within a supplementary annotation box with 24 point type.

5. Sequence the slides and perform a copy edit on the entire set, adjusting wording to insure consistency between slides and exercises sheets.

6. Pilot test the training with a small initial group and publish the slides at the group's web site for optional download by learners. Refine the slides and exercises as dictated by this experience before releasing them for widespread use.

Conclusions

It has been our experience that the product and method for its development which grew out of our research effort has enabled our relatively small group of trainer materials developers to create our needed materials with appropriate content in minimal timeframes. After assuming responsibilities for this training with the 2007 calendar year we have successfully conducted an average of three weekly sessions throughout the academic year covering an expanding set of software. The clear emphasis on learner work-product outcomes and the front-end design incorporated into this process has made it possible to parcel out development work on the same course between multiple trainer developers yet still achieve a consistent product when the parts are joined together. A given three-hour training course with five to ten short exercises may require as little as two weeks to develop through the pilot test stage, which has proven to be a boon to the rapidly-evolving software and training needs of the university as peaks arise during the academic year.

Future Improvements and Research

Several additional developments in this area suggest themselves. One which is nearing the point of implementation is the use of the Notes feature of Powerpoint to add a small amount of explanatory verbiage to slide sets themselves, which would be ignored during the use of the slides and exercises for instructor-led training but could useful to self-guided learners. This would in effect completely reverse the traditional manual based training materials paradigm because the "manual" would be the last product developed rather than the first. The lack of traditional training manual materials has not handicapped our efforts in the two years since we assumed responsibility for this area but manuals may yet be of assistance to self-paced learners and to our own staff as turnover occurs.

Formal research to assess the utility of our existing efforts and gauge the outcomes of this additional documentation effort are in the planning stages.

An additional area of extension lies in the provision of audio annotation for the slide sets, to (perhaps) further improve their utility and usability. Methods to accomplish this are under evaluation including the overarching question of whether the audio need be tied to the slide presentation or completely separate and free-standing, given the software tradeoffs and flexibility, or lack of flexibility, of each approach.

Development of a method to organize short segments of learning in a web-based "how to" reference is also on the agenda, to serve both our user community and the university help desk. Pilot testing of a simple method to produce the HTML necessary for such a site is underway.

19

Staff Development In Distance Education: The Evolution Of One Approach

Abstract

The International Extension College (IEC), UK, and Kyambogo University (KU), Uganda, are working together on a training programme for KU's ODL staff, using an ODL model. This paper discusses the pedagogical and technical approach of the programme. It also examines the reasons for the success of this collaborative venture and presents lessons for the future.

Staff Development in ODL

There are plenty of ODL institutions which provide fulltime or on-the-job training for their staff. Interestingly, however, there don't seem to be many prominent examples of institutions which use ODL for staff training and development. The Indira Gandhi National Open University in India is an honourable exception. So is CDEP (Southern Africa), which is a programme for staff of institutions in more than one country. As a regional course, CDEP has succeeded in modelling good ODL practice and promoting a learner centred approach. [Not surprisingly, isolated or remote CDEP learners have experienced problems with delivery of the course services and have suffered from lack of support. But the providers are committed to addressing these issues and improving the course's coverage and usefulness, as well as the recognition and reward offered to those who complete it successfully.

There is a small literature on staff development in ODL. Reviewing it raises the question whether ODL is an underused approach to training. The UKOU, for example, doesn't use ODL for staff development (Sewart, 1998, 149). Lentell's regular staff development column in *Open praxis* for 10 years from 1993 never examined it, though she took some swipes at the cookbook approach to training manuals. Rather few of the contributors to Latchem & Lockwood (1998) deal with ODL as a tool for staff development. An exception is Gunn & Panko, who describe a staff development course using self-study.

What Randell & Bitzer say about South Africa is true more widely: 'Overcoming years of reinforcement of a teacher-focused model of teaching and learning and changing underlying conceptions of learning and teaching will be a lengthy process requiring a great deal of skilful professional development.' The needs in many other developing countries are the same.

Course and materials developers need to be enabled to develop programmes which encourage deep and autonomic learning and which are culturally and linguistically appropriate. Tutors and counsellors need to acquire new student-centred approaches to teaching and learning and develop their diagnostic, problem-solving and inter-personal skills in assisting culturally diverse students. Managers and administrators need to be given the knowledge and ability to provide and evaluate relevant support systems for staff'.

Lentell (1994) identifies an important tension between what tutors and managers look for in staff development.

On the one hand, practitioners demand the development of a professional learning community, i.e. a learning organisation. On the other, distance education managers have seen their major task as 'to brief and train tutors in a new mode of delivery and not to encourage ongoing learning'. 'Failure to address this contradiction will lead to a cynicism among staff and a sense that the language of staff development is merely empty rhetoric'.

Dillon and Walsh, in a review of the distance education journal literature, concluded that 'faculty [teaching staff] development programmes designed to promote distance teaching are concerned primarily with training and do little to encourage or support a dramatic restructuring of faculty roles'.

They identified the issue of learner ownership, for which such change in academic culture is necessary, as central to the development and successful diffusion of distance education.

IEC'S EXPERIENCE

IEC is a small British educational non-governmental organisation that was established in 1971 for the purpose of using distance education to benefit people not provided for in mainstream education in developing countries. Its core activity is the provision of consultancy, training, information and technical support to institutions, governments and projects, in the design, development, delivery and evaluation of open and distance learning (ODL) programmes.

IEC can claim always to have recognised that distance educators need to experience distance education from the learner's perspective to fully understand their roles. Its training manuals were offered as correspondence courses more than twenty years ago. Fifteen years ago it developed a print plus audio international MA in Distance Education for the University of London, and also used this experience in putting together a series of training toolkits for distance educators for the Commonwealth of Learning and the Asian Development Bank.

IEC has also participated in very many residential courses run by individual programmes and providers over the years. But our own introduction to distance education course, *Distance education for development* (DED), was always run face-to-face in London for over twenty years. This reflected the importance of participants learning from each other and IEC learning from the participants. During this time we frequently revised and reorganised both our content and our delivery. Improvements were based mainly on our own experience and participants' feedback. Despite offering higher level staff development programmes at a distance, IEC had not so far bitten the bullet of developing a distance version of DED.

IEC is currently collaborating with the Department of Distance Education at Kyambogo University in a capacity building support project for teacher education at a distance. This is a five-year human resource development (HRD) programme, with funding from the Nuffield Foundation, which began in April 2001. It includes a print-based ODL course for staff coming to ODL for the first time, developed by IEC and managed, tutored and assessed by KU.

KU plays the leading role in teacher education in Uganda, with responsibility for matters relating to teacher training throughout the country. It provides pre-service and in-service training, and works with teachers' colleges to develop curricula and improve standards of education. One of its training programmes is an in-service primary teachers' diploma programme delivered at a distance, the Diploma in Education Primary External (DEPE). KU sets examinations, awards certificates and diplomas, and serves as a resource centre for education services, research and publications.

A course called *Introduction to distance education* is part of the HRD programme. It is designed to introduce the practice of ODL to managers and lecturers in Ugandan Primary Teachers' Colleges (PTCs), National Teachers' Colleges (NTCs) and KU, who are involved in the delivery of DEPE. The aim is to reach as many as possible of those involved in ODL or likely to be interested in it for teacher education, in order to increase the size of the pool of trained people available to develop the ODL work of KU.

The idea of offering a one-year ODL course emerged from an initial training needs assessment workshop. Offering the course by correspondence and faceto- face makes it possible to combine KU's resources in Uganda with IEC's already developed curriculum. A course consisting of three modules, delivered over a period of three terms to coincide with school terms, was specially developed, on the basis of DED. The first cohort took the course from January 2002; the second started in February 2004.

We assumed that:

- with the requisite skills KU would be able to do a more professional job with its current ODL courses and be able to extend the number and type of courses it can offer
- and that the use of ODL would:
- motivate the participants to learn
- encourage the functioning of learning circles
- teach participants to empathise with their students.

We designed the programme to minimise the risks of failure by:

- incorporating in-country support from PTCs

- involving past learners on IEC courses and experienced distance educators as tutors
- integrating face-to-face sessions into the delivery model
- enabling new knowledge and skills to be put to immediate use (a benefit even for non-completers).

Cross-cultural transfer was an issue. 'Staff development for distance education needs to be sensitive to the fact that learner autonomy may be valued differently by the teacher's and learners' respective cultures' (Matthewson & Thaman, 1998, 119-120). The materials for this course were created by writers familiar with teacher education in Uganda, and were pretested by Ugandans.

Delivery, support to and administration of the programme are handled in country by the Coordinator and a small team of Ugandan tutors, all of whom had had previous training experience in ODL. Tutors receive further induction to the course as it progresses. The initial training of trainers was undertaken by IEC, but subsequent sessions were facilitated by the Coordinator. Now that the one-year course is being repeated, the Coordinator is leading all the training himself.

Following the mid-term external evaluation (see below), funds were diverted from the overseas training budget, which would have benefited two people directly, to running the one year distance course for a further 50 participants, as a more effective use of resources.

The Approach

Our approach with this course is consistent with that of Haigh, who describes his approach to staff development in open and flexible learning as offering a 'self-directed learning package'. But he uses ODL only at the outset, and prefers to work face-to-face for further exploration. What he says about setting a modest agenda certainly corresponds with the thinking of our course developers.

I observe that 'getting practical experience' needs to be a priority when we are novices, because it is from experience that we will learn many of the important things to do with using skills well. Often I need to resist my inclination as an enthusiastic teacher to overwhelm them with a surfeit of 'good ideas that they could try out' particularly ideas that will not be fully meaningful when they lack experiences to relate them to. Whether all our course participants would agree that we set a modest agenda is not so clear. But the overwhelming message from the evaluations of the course, which we come to below, is that they relished the challenges of both new approaches and new knowledge.

We believed that first hand experience of what it is like to study at a distance would provide the best understanding of learners' material, support and delivery needs. Trainers, tutors, lecturers, college principals and administrators who have experienced ODL themselves are likely to empathise much more with their students, and will be better informed when it comes to design and delivery of suitable courses. This was demonstrated in earlier experience in Uganda, when IEC raised funds to enable teacher educators in the NITEP project to study at a distance at postgraduate diploma level as well as in IEC collaborations in other countries. In each case a group of staff enrolled on courses from the University of London External MA in Distance Education. The learners worked independently but with peer group support and were very successful in maintaining study and achieving good results. In the KU project it was possible to take this a stage further and develop a course designed for the specific needs of a relatively homogeneous group of teacher educators, all working in the same ODL programme.

Application

The course was designed so that participants would be in a position to put what they had learned in to practice immediately. Wherever possible examples and activities draw on the day-to-day experience of the participants, making the learning highly relevant and practical.

In this way the training programmes offered by KU can be updated and improved on a continuing basis and with immediate impact. For example, the assignment in the materials development module is to evaluate sample materials from KU's Diploma in Education Primary External (DEPE). The Assistant ODL Coordinator collected together all the critiques produced by the first batch of learners to collate and analyse, in order to make revisions to these materials.

Many course participants commented on the power of evaluating their own materials:

> especially the writers who seem to have accepted the evaluation with good humour and humility. The materials they reviewed had up to then been a source of some pride, so this was a real eye opener.

The learning is spaced out to give time for lessons learned to be put into practice and takes into account people's capacity to absorb new ideas and techniques. Skills and ideas are reinforced through the residential sessions and the variety of learning experiences offered, as well as by colleagues who are also learning. Reaching a larger number of learners through ODL means that there are more colleagues with a shared understanding of the topics with whom to interact.

Technology

Although KU is the lead institution for teacher education in Uganda, its funding is not adequate for any significant investment in technology. Its registry still uses a paper based record system which often proves inefficient, as documents get lost or are difficult to find.

DDE has been dependent on the HRD project for a small amount of computer equipment and Internet connectivity, though KU is in the process of taking over these costs. It is still unthinkable that DDE should use the Internet to download materials or for interactive learning with teachers. What connectivity there is with some PTCs, and it is minimal, is made available to DEPE trainees during face-to-face sessions. Teachers living and working

within reach of these PTCs may also get some access during term time. The one-year ODL course in fact uses a delivery system very similar to KU's DEPE programme: printed modules and face-to-face residential sessions. The choice of this low tech approach has to be seen in the context of connectivity in Uganda.

The advance of the mobile telephone is making communication possible without so much travelling as in the past. KU's Department of Distance Education (DDE) is actively seeking ways to use this technology to benefit its students.

EVALUATION

The mid-term review of the HRD programme undertaken on behalf of the funder concluded.

The one year course has been the single most important activity of the project so far. Virtually all of those enrolled (tutors, administrators, PTC and NTC principals and others involved in DE) completed the course. It appears to have been a really exciting and transforming experience inspiring people, making them realise from their own experience just what learners need, and bringing people together in peer groups and experiencing a level of support that has had a profound effect on many of those I talked to. In addition to the skills and learning, many also cited the experience of peer group support as a major element of the course, which may also have had the additional benefit of building relationships and teamwork throughout what is essentially a decentralised operation. People had been kept going through family crises – and in one case a serious accident a really powerful sense of support which it was clear several people still missed. In terms of capacity building activities as a whole [the Head of KU's DDE, and project coordinator] noted that the one year course was far more cost effective than funding 10 individuals for further [fulltime academic] study. They are few, difficult to choose and the effect is isolated, in contrast to the effect of the course.

The course is the key part. It puts people in the customer's shoes a complete reversal which has had a very powerful effect. Effectively the course has been a Trojan horse bringing about major cultural changes in attitudes and practice as well as skills. I was also struck by the way this is a complex decentralised organisational change experience and one which would be useful to monitor and learn from a systems change perspective as well as from the distance learning perspective.

Our own evaluation, based on stakeholders, tutors and 49 learners' returns, independently came to many of the same conclusions. The distance study course seems to have been of particular value in the sharing together of the ups and downs of isolated study and the camaraderie of the face-to-face tutorials and workshops. These brought together people from diverse jobs and locations with a unifying interest in teacher education. This experience of peer group support seems to lay down a strong foundation on which to improve and promote ODL for teacher education in Uganda.

This form of training has proved so successful and popular that the course is being run again for a further 50 learners. It is worth noting that running the course for a second cohort brings the cost per learner down significantly. If funds were available for a third cohort, it would fall further still.

This is not to say that the course was cheap. It would have been possible to reach the same number through intensive short workshops for a similar cost. But it would not have been possible to provide the depth of knowledge in that time, or to enable participants to apply the skills so effectively to their working lives; nor would they have enjoyed the first hand experience of being ODL students. Future research, as planned by KU, into the impact of the course will further elucidate its real value, but from the evidence available so far it seems to be a cost-effective programme of training.

LESSONS

In ODL, inter-institutional collaboration is increasing in importance. Sharing the costs of course development through co-development, sales and leasing arrangements makes sense. However, as Spronk observes, such collaboration is by no means easy to establish or maintain. Trust and respect are crucial for all those involved. In our case, KU and IEC already had a good relationship and there was a desire in both to cooperate further. And the HRD project was designed to build on the relationship and to be flexible.

'Multilateral collaboration [in staff development] may be problematic but long-term bilateral relations serve well. In addition, both partners recognised the importance of:

- the receptiveness of this group of learners, as compared with many academics (Abdullah, 1998: 87)

- judging the appropriateness of the methods and content: 'What is modern in one context is already dated, or outdated, in another, and only a dream for the future in yet another. With a relatively small clientele and pragmatic projections for human-resource requirements, *participatory* models emphasising more *reflective* approaches may be employed.
- emphasising and demonstrating the critical importance of learner support: 'many support functions are taken for granted by faculty and students accustomed to on-campus classes. Distance education programme developed need to ensure that their students not only have access to those, but also to... technical and logistical support, psycho-social or affective support and tutorial counselling mentoring support'.
- validation by evaluation.

We had the advantage of starting with a curriculum which had evolved over time and space. But we still managed to generate the familiar problem of student overload in the self-study part of the course, particularly by setting demanding and time consuming assignments. Face-to-face work is crucially important, but so too are the (also familiar) problems of money, transport and accommodation. 'Under these circumstances, programmes that are as flexible as possible in allowing students to work with others, catch up on late assignments, or receive extra help from the instructor are going to be the most successful in helping students to achieve their goals.

It was not always possible to deliver all aspects of the distance study course on time. Delays in the shipment of materials, and in the receipt of funds by the local bank and approval for release of funds from the KU accounts, led to the postponement of one or two activities. These were also useful learning experiences for the participants - knowing first hand what not to do can also be powerful. One of DDE's current targets is to improve logistics.

THE FUTURE

The human resource development project with KU is, at the time of writing, half way through its implementation. There are a number of pointers towards what is making change possible in KU. The indications are that the most important of these has been the empathetic experience of learning about ODL by doing it: by studying at a distance. A second cohort is studying the materials this year and research has been commissioned that will consider the impact of the first run of the course on its participants' professional lives and the organisation of ODL in their institutions. It will be possible to return to this programme to consider the impact of this method (and content) of training on change at KU and to see whether we can confirm the conclusions drawn so far. We would like to find a way of offering people who complete this course some kind of accredited certificate which would count towards a recognised qualification. This is an issue that came up in our evaluation, and which needs to be pursued. At the same time as this course is being offered to a clearly defined group of educators in one country, IEC is working on ways of making the same basic curriculum available more widely. Organisations in other developing countries have approached us about running a version of it for similar groups. And we are actively involved in developing with the Institute of Education in London a course to replace the original residential DED. This will be delivered internationally using a low cost strategy and appropriate technologies - probably print with email tutorial support, and the option for students to work together using email contact.

20

Training and Development in the Civil Service

Introduction

While the role and ethos of the civil service has remained intact since the foundation of the State, the environment within which it operates has changed fundamentally as a result of economic growth, national and international political developments and global scientific and technological advances. These have led to new Government policies in social, political and economic matters. The effectiveness with which the new policies are implemented is largely dependent on the quality of civil service administration and the ability of its staff to operate effectively in the changed environment.

The demand for high calibre staff in the civil service has coincided with growing problems in their retention and recruitment, especially those with technical and professional expertise and those with specific experience. International studies suggest that job satisfaction and opportunities for personal development are important factors in countering this problem. These factors and recent developments in the area of staff performance management have increased the importance of training and development in the overall context of human resource management in the civil service.

The growing importance of training and development is reflected in the growth in expenditure in this area in recent years, amounting to £16.5 million in 1999. The recent increase in target expenditure to 4% of payroll indicates that spending on training and development is set to accelerate further in the coming years.

The examination set out to review training and development activity across the civil service with a view to assessing how it could be improved in terms of its organisation, management and overall effectiveness.

Administrative Framework

Departments are responsible for meeting the training needs of their staff while the Department of Finance provides corporate support across the civil service for management training and development.

A policy statement dedicated to training and development in the civil service as a whole does not exist. There are different approaches to policies and planning at departmental level. While most have articulated strategies on training and development, many do not have training policies, plans and review procedures.

Training needs analysis is limited and this, in turn, affects the quality of planning and the effectiveness of training provided. A detailed and considered statement of policy on civil service training and development as a whole is desirable as it would provide a standard framework for the production of local policies and plans.

A survey of departments indicated that most are satisfied with the level of corporate support they receive for specific civil service policy initiatives, but there are contrasting views on the service provided in regard to the dissemination of training and development best practice. The training function in many departments is headed by staff at middle management level. The distance from the top increases the risk that training will not receive adequate management attention. This problem can be addressed by ensuring that training and development is regularly on the agenda of top management meetings.

Training and Development Resources

There are considerable differences between civil service departments in the amount of resources allocated to training and development and in the way these resources are managed. Departments have different operating requirements and their disparate approaches to training and development reflect the varying needs to be addressed.

Departments tend not to review the performance of trainers, whether they be civil servants or contracted in from the private sector. Although there are some opportunities to achieve economies through co-operation and sharing facilities between departments, in practice, potential savings were generally not realised. The target expenditure for training and development by departments has recently been raised even though the average actual expenditure in 1999 was some way short of the original target, indicating that departments have difficulty, at present, in absorbing more resources. These findings suggest the need for better planning and management of training and development resources, a need which is likely to become more pressing with the advent of performance management and the subsequent increase in demand for training and development.

Training Provided

Informal or on-the-job training is an important source of training and development and is used widely across the civil service. However, it is treated as part of normal working hours and is not recorded separately. The introduction of performance management is likely to lead to the formal recognition of this type of training. The average number of formal training days received each year by civil servants compares well to that received in the private sector. However, considerable differences exist between departments in the average number of training days received by staff and, in general, there is less training and development provided to civil servants in the highest and lowest grades.

By far the largest proportion of civil service training and development is in the technical area. Training and development dealing with roles, attitudes and behaviours is consistently less in evidence, suggesting an absence of appreciation, at corporate and departmental level, of the value of this type of training as a means of improving performance.

The delivery of foreign language training in the civil service has recently been rationalised. The reasons for a drop-out rate of approximately 50% on foreign language courses need to be established.

Top Management Training

Given their importance to the organisation, private sector companies devote considerable energy to the training and development of top managers and their successors. However, the civil service largely relies on networks, seminars and conferences for top management training and development and lacks a specific programme in this area. A separate development programme which takes account of the particular requirements and circumstances of top managers should be developed, implemented and evaluated.

Management Information Systems

Many departments were unable to respond fully to the data requirements of the examination, indicating weaknesses in their management information systems. This had the effect of restricting the scope of the examination's data analysis. However, new information systems are currently being introduced across departments and are expected to deal with this problem.

The expenditure target of 4% of payroll is used as the sole indicator of and mechanism for calculating the investment by departments in training and development. There is a need to develop more effective performance indicators and to develop a better model for calculating the level of investment by departments in training and development.

Evaluation

Expert analysis at an international level suggests that much investment in training and development is wasted as programmes do not succeed in delivering the expected outcomes. The evaluation systems used by the civil service at present are limited in their effectiveness. Although the importance of evaluation needs to be balanced against the cost involved, the civil service needs to establish proper evaluation systems if it is to be effective in assessing whether its training and development programmes are meeting the objectives set for them.

Performance Management and Development System

The most significant recent change in the civil service has been the introduction of the Performance Management & Development System (PMDS). Focused on improving skills and performance, the new system will change the way civil servants are managed and is expected to have important implications for training and development.

The Department of Finance expects that the shortcomings identified in this report will be addressed with the introduction of the PMDS. International experience suggests that, notwithstanding a new approach to training and development, existing weaknesses will persist unless regular review takes place.

Conclusions and Recommendations

The civil service needs to continue its move from a mindset of seeing training and development as a cost to one of seeing it as an investment. The PMDS is expected to deliver much of this change. It should be underpinned by the following.

- A central policy on civil service training and development should be formulated to provide overall direction and guidance.
- Reliable management information systems should be designed to enable training and development to be monitored and evaluated at departmental level and across the civil service as a whole.
- Needs analysis should be introduced which is focused on the training and development which will provide the outcome needed to support objectives.
- The specific needs of top managers should be identified and training and development programmes designed which are appropriate and of value to these managers.
- More consistent support for the training and development function needs to be articulated by senior managers and their action to implement this support should be subject to independent scrutiny.
- Departments should introduce comprehensive evaluation systems based on measuring the effectiveness of training in terms of business outputs and outcomes.
- Benchmarking and systems for independent accreditation should be used to verify performance.

While the role and ethos of the civil service has remained intact since the foundation of the State, the environment within which it operates has changed fundamentally. It is now generally recognised that the satisfactory performance of civil service administration depends on how well it adapts to an operating environment which is highly competitive, technologically sophisticated, globalized in perspective and changing with unprecedented pace, depth and variety.

To meet these challenges a range of new policies have emerged in recent years to improve strategic planning and the delegation of authority and to introduce greater transparency and accountability and improved customer service.

In common with many organisations, the civil service is experiencing significant problems in staff recruitment and retention. International research suggests that opportunities for continuous development are a key incentive in recruiting and retaining staff.

Within the last 12 months the finalisation of the arrangements for the introduction of the new Performance Management and Development System (PMDS) has the potential for significant development of human resource management across the civil service, particularly in the area of training and development. The commitment to the PMDS is evidence of the importance now attached to the management and development of staff in the civil service.

Training and Development

Training and development activities are important elements of the human resource management function of an organisation.

Training is a planned and systematic activity, through learning experiences, to impart knowledge or develop individual or group skills and attitudes for the purpose of improving performance. Effective training would focus on the needs of the organisation, would be delivered over a relatively short timescale and should result in immediate improvement of performance.

Development is long term in nature and is more concerned with maximising an individual's potential. It is focused on the needs of both the individual and the organisation. It involves coaching, counselling, mentoring, guidance and third level education programmes. Development should result in improved competence in the capabilities of the individual in areas such as management, decision making and problem solving. Development programmes are often geared towards preparing individuals to take up future more senior roles in an organisation.

Training and development are complementary parts of the same process. They are interlinked and interdependent, rather than sequential and hierarchical.

Each Government department1 is responsible for the training and development of its staff and has an annual training budget which is used to provide in-house training and or procure it externally. Departments appoint Departmental Training Officers, generally at Assistant Principal Higher Executive Officer level, who have a particular responsibility for staff training in respect of grades up to and including Executive Officer. Many departments have dedicated training units which provide or procure courses for staff at these and higher levels. Some departments, for example Revenue and Social, Community and Family Affairs, have a substantial internal training function.

At the overall civil service level, training and development support is provided by the Centre for Management and Organisation Development (CMOD) in the Department of Finance. CMOD, which embraces the former Civil Service Training Centre, organises and delivers a range of courses and conferences, directed at the management grades of Higher Executive Officer and upwards, which address common and corporate management development needs and which are open to all departments.

CMOD assists also with training needs analysis in individual departments. It supports and facilitates networks for key groups such as Assistant Secretaries, Principal Officers, Personnel Officers, Finance Officers, Women Managers, Internal Auditors and Departmental Training Officers. These networks were set up in the late 1980s and early 1990s and are a means for officers at these levels to identify and address issues of common concern including training and development needs.

With the advent of the Strategic Management Initiative (SMI) in the civil service in the early 1990s, there has been a renewed focus on staff training and development in the context of business needs and objectives which are now articulated through departments' periodic Statements of Strategy and annual business plans under the SMI process. This focus was reinforced by *Delivering Better Government* which, inter alia, set a target of an annual expenditure of at least 3% of payroll on staff training and development. This target was to be reached over the lifetime of Partnership 2000. The *Programme for Prosperity and Fairness* raises the target to 4% of payroll by 2003. The new PMDS, which is now being implemented, should enhance further the focus on staff training and development and the link to business and organisational needs and objectives.

Expenditure on Training and Development

Expenditure on training and development in the civil service has increased steadily in the last ten years. Figure

1.1 shows estimated non-salary expenditure, including the cost of external trainers, refund of fees, cost of seminars and conferences directly related to training, purchase of training materials, rental cost of training facilities and the cost of administrative support, for the period 1991 to 1999. Full expenditure, including in-house trainers' salaries and expenditure by CMOD, is shown for the period 1997 to 1999. Data on these costs are not available prior to 1997. Full expenditure on civil service training and development for 1999 amounted to £16.5 million (Appendix D).

Apart altogether from the direct cost of training, there are considerable opportunity costs arising out of staff attendance at training courses.

Value for Money Issues in Training and Development

The effectiveness of the training and development function will typically depend on how well it is integrated into the strategy and business planning process of a department and how well it is supported by top management.

The delivery of value for money from training and development activity requires that specific policies, strategies and plans should be developed by departments for the training and development function. Each department should establish a framework outlining the role, position and responsibilities of the training function. It should include specific training objectives that arise from an analysis of the department's needs and identify the criteria to be used to assess performance. The framework should also include a training plan which sets out the resources available and how they will be used.

An examination of value for money issues associated with training and development is usually based on an analysis of inputs, activities, outputs and outcomes. The relationships between these elements is shown in Figure

Training and development inputs are the resources required to enable the organisation to implement its training plans. An organisation is achieving economy when it has the optimum quality of resources in place at the best price. Training and development resources include staff, budgets and training facilities.

For the purpose of this examination, efficient training and development was considered in terms of optimising the amount and quality of training delivered to staff. The assessment of efficiency includes identifying who receives training and assessing the nature and extent of training delivered.

To be effective, a training and development programme should be appropriate to the objectives identified in the planning process and should result in the expected improvement in performance.

Scope and Objectives of the Examination

The overall objective of the examination was to review the economy and efficiency of training and development activity across the civil service and to consider the systems, practices and procedures used to assess effectiveness.

Each Government department is responsible for carrying out the operations vested by law in the Minister and for managing and administering the resources allocated for this purpose. However, they are subject to common codes and regulations and to general co-ordination by the Department of Finance, which exercises a degree

Objective To improve performance and productivity

Inputs Financial, human, organisational

Resources allocated to resources required to carry out training produce an output and development

Output Trained and Developed Staff

The product of a process or that which results from processing inputs

Outcome Improved performance

The ultimate effect or consequence of an action or process

of central control over civil service policy on financial and staffing matters. The examination considers training and development in the civil service as a whole, with departments identified as constituent parts for the purpose of illustration and analysis.

The examination reviews training and development practice as it applies to general service grades and allied grades common to two or more departments. It covers all Government departments and is principally concerned with the specific details of training and development undertaken in the period 1997 to 1999.

A full range of training data from departments for a number of years would allow the identification of trends and analysis of developments. However, following the issue of a pilot questionnaire and discussions with a number of departments, it became clear that data was not available on a sufficiently widespread basis to allow for such analysis. The necessary data could only be provided for 1998 and 1999, which did not allow for a longitudinal study as envisaged. Consequently, the figures in the report are for 1999 unless otherwise stated.

While it is recognised that coaching and on-the-job training have an important part to play in improving performance and fostering development, departments do not keep records of such training. Consequently, the examination was confined to formal training and development programmes. These include in-house or external training courses, seminars and workshops, and programmes which support formal education leading to academic and professional qualifications.

Methodology

The examination was carried out by staff of the Office of the Comptroller and Auditor General with assistance from consultants. The nature and extent of training and development in the civil service was established by means of a survey of all Government departments4. The survey was conducted through

- the issue of a questionnaire to three departments on a pilot basis to clarify issues and enable the questionnaire to be revised to ensure that all relevant data was sought and obtained
- discussions with relevant officials in Government departments and in some private sector organisations
- the issue of the revised questionnaire to all departments to gather information on their training and development policies, procedures, costs and effectiveness (the questionnaire results are given in Appendices B and C)
- assessment of the results of the questionnaire and conclusions to be drawn from the data.

The examination also involved

- visits to four departments for more detailed analysis
- examination of training and development policies and practices in selected comparable private sector organisations (detailed analysis at Appendix A)
- assessment of the role and function of CMOD, which is part of the Department

of Finance, in relation to training and development in the civil service

- review of expenditure data on training and development submitted annually by departments to CMOD
- review of the training and development policies and practices in the UK civil service.

Structure of the Report

The report structure adopted follows the operational life cycle of planning, implementation and evaluation and the value for money input-output model deals with the objectives of training and development and analyses the strategic and administrative framework for management support of these objectives. Consider the economy of inputs and resources and the efficiency of output, respectively. Chapter 5 examines the systems, practices and procedures in place for evaluating training and development outcomes.

Setting The Framework

The achievement of value for money from investment in training and development depends to a large extent on the strength of the framework under which civil service training and development activities take place. The framework includes the policy and planning processes and the systems for analysing training needs and for collecting relevant management information.

This chapter divides the existing framework into two parts. The existence of policy objectives for training and development for the civil service as a whole and at departmental level is first considered. The impact of the new PMDS is highlighted. The chapter then examines the framework for strategy and planning of training and development activities using the following criteria

- Training needs analysis
- Use of CMOD5
- Management information
- Top level support

Training and Development Policies

The examination found that where civil service-wide policy on training is articulated, it is usually done as part of a large scale programme, such as the PMDS and usually in the context of supporting the introduction of the programme.

For example, under the *Programme for Prosperity and Fairness,* "the Civil Service is committed to enhanced training and development for management and staff at all levels in the context of implementing and developing the performance management and development system, ensuring better quality in service delivery and enhancing policy analysis, development and implementation."

A detailed and considered statement of policy, dedicated solely to training and development for the civil service as a whole, does not exist.

Policy on training and development at departmental level is somewhat disjointed. Some departments have produced their own training and development policies. According to the survey responses from departments, five departments have a formal policy on continuing development for professional and technical staff, six have a policy on staff rotation, three have a policy on staff exchanges and secondments and three have policies on coaching and mentoring newly appointed or promoted staff.

The Department of Finance considers that it is questionable whether a detailed statement of policy or strategic plan for civil service training and development as a whole would serve a useful purpose. The Department draws attention to the high level statements of policy contained in *Partnership 2000* and *The Programme for Prosperity and Fairness* as helpful to setting the overall thrust and general parameters within which individual departments should develop their own strategies.

The Department considers that, prior to the Strategic Management Initiative (SMI), a coherent policy on civil service training and development was articulated centrally through CMOD's annual Management Development Programme. The Programme detailed centrally available courses and other support services and set out the general thrust and context of civil service training and development. In more recent years, with the introduction of SMI, individual departments produce statements of strategy and business plans with the consequence of a more targeted focus on training and development. Details of the programme of courses are now issued electronically by CMOD every six months.

However, the variety of approaches by departments, as suggested by the survey data in general, indicates that a separate civil service-wide policy statement on implementing training and development is desirable as it would provide a standard framework for the production of local policies and plans. Such a statement should be broad enough to allow implementation to be tailored to the specific needs of departments, while sufficiently detailed to ensure they stay within overall civil service objectives.

The Performance Management and Development System

In 1996, the SMI report *Delivering Better Government - A Programme of Change for the Irish Civil Service* recognised the need for a new approach to human resource management, particularly the introduction of performance management systems which would ensure that staff had the competencies and skills required to deliver a department's strategies and objectives. The report recognised that this would involve identifying the particular skills and competencies needed by departments and individuals and providing the necessary framework and resources to enable these skills and competencies to be developed.

To implement this programme, departments were to prepare staff development plans based on competencies, skills and human resource strategies. Each department was to raise its expenditure on training and development from an average of less than 0.75% to at least 3% of payroll costs. Although, on average, departmental expenditure had only reached 2.1% of payroll costs by 1999, or 2.3% including CMOD expenditure

The PMDS is the most recent of the SMI programmes and is designed to improve overall performance throughout the civil service. It is based on role profiles setting out objectives and the key skills and competencies needed to realise those objectives. Each member of staff is required to have the necessary competencies to do the job to which he or she is assigned. If the person lacks one or more of these competencies, then he or she should receive whatever training and development is required to become proficient in that area.

The linking of training and development to the PMDS is significant as it recognises the importance of training and development as part of the overall approach to better human resource management in the civil service. Initial efforts are being directed towards a training programme concerned with explaining the various roles involved in the PMDS and providing guidance on how to operate the system. The real potential of the new system is the opportunity it provides to customise departmental training and development expenditure to the individual staff development needs which training policies will be designed to fulfil. This would represent a fundamental shift from the traditional view of training and development as a (sometimes avoidable) cost towards the new approach of considering it as an investment in people.

The New Zealand public service underwent fundamental reform in the late 1980s. The reforms were intended to shift the focus to outputs and outcomes and towards managing operational and strategic performance accordingly. Progress reviews some years later indicated that some problems remained to be overcome. The findings, summarised in llustrate the value of carrying out a review of reforms introduced to the Irish civil service, such as the PMDS, to ensure they are effective in delivering the results expected.

- departments still tended to focus on immediate rather than long-term needs
- insufficient attention was given to investment in human capital
- Human resource management (HRM) planning was not aligned with business planning and in most areas there was a lack of sound and comprehensive information required for strategic HRM
- existing information systems did not provide adequate information on current skills and likely skills gaps
- skills shortages were reported in areas of strategic and conceptual thinking, analytical skills, economic and financial analytical skills, HRM, contract management, quality assurance, information

technology and operational management

- management standards within departments were very low and management development would need to be linked to required competencies
- there was a limited supply of suitable candidates for chief executive positions implying too little investment in senior management development
- a key issue in the retention of staff was the dwindling resources to train and develop staff and the absence of a service-wide approach to developing staff.

Strategy and Planning

The examination set out to assess whether training and development is seen as an integral part of the achievement of civil service objectives, or whether it is seen as an administrative function and treated as peripheral to their achievement. The importance of training and development is indicated by whether it is managed on an *ad hoc* basis, or whether it is driven by formal planning and management systems.

The quality of training and development planning at departmental level was assessed on a range of criteria. Specific questions were asked in the survey about the existence of training plans, systems for analysing training needs, annual reviews of training activities and annual reports on the outcome.

The responses indicated that some departments take a comprehensive approach, while others satisfy one or two of the criteria. 73% of departments include specific objectives and strategies for staff training and development in their statements of strategy. While most departments have articulated a strategy on training and development, only 54% have a formal training plan and only 43% have training committees. Less than a quarter combine planning with an annual review and a training report. Some departments keep records but do not have formal planning, annual review or annual reports.

The results indicate that departments articulate the importance of training and development at a high strategic level but, in many cases, the follow through at operational level is not as cohesive.

Training Needs Analysis

If training is about bridging the gap between individual and organisational competencies, a training unit needs to have up to date information regarding the knowledge and skills deficit of staff throughout the organisation. The best way of acquiring this information is to conduct a comprehensive training needs analysis.

Training needs analysis is a systematic and comprehensive process which assesses the business goals of the organisation, determines the training needs required to achieve those goals and decides the training priorities which will make the greatest contribution to the organisation. The process ensures that training and development resources can be planned to meet valid need.

In the survey, departments were asked about training needs analysis to establish if the training provided is based on the actual needs of the department and its staff.

Departments were also asked about the use of competencies as a guide to training and development needs and the role of line managers in determining such needs.

Training needs analysis is referred to in the published strategy statements of many departments but the practice of carrying out the analysis varies. The survey results indicate that needs identification procedures are limited in most departments and consultation tends to be informal.

Only 39% of the departments surveyed had carried out a formal analysis since January 1997. The survey revealed the following variety of approaches to identifying training needs.

- Core skills and competencies are used by 50% of departments to identify their staff training needs. However, the annual staff appraisal process is used by only 25% of departments for this purpose.
- Representative groups of staff and managers are used by 75% of departments, but only 29% surveyed all staff in the target group.
- Line managers in 59% of departments surveyed are consulted on training needs, but they complete questionnaires in only 18% of departments.
- For departments that prepared a training needs analysis, 42% engaged the assistance of external consultants while 58% carried out the analysis internally.

The survey results show that, of the departments which did not carry out a formal needs analysis, the majority (64%) did not have a formal training plan.

Some training officers are reluctant to conduct a comprehensive analysis of all staff training needs in case it should raise unrealistic expectations that cannot be met.

Other trainers have stated that they did not proceed with a full training needs analysis of the staff in their department because of the imminent introduction of the PMDS into the civil service.

The introduction of the PMDS will provide a major challenge to training units in departments as there will be a clear link between competency identification per task and grade and the training effort required to up-skill staff accordingly. In these circumstances, a formal needs analysis will be essential for an objective assessment of the competencies and skills required to lift the overall performance of the individual and the department.

The Department of Finance considers that the introduction of PMDS will provide a comprehensive overview of the training and development needs at individual, team and organisation level and will do so within an overall civil service framework.

The examination set out to assess the corporate nature of the training function, that is the extent to which departments see themselves as part of a bigger organisation, the civil service. The assessment was based on questions related to the central management and/or support of civil service training and development.

As a division of the Department of Finance, CMOD's function is to provide a unified, co-ordinated approach to the delivery of advisory and support services to the civil service in the areas of information technology, staff development and management, and organisation systems development. Its mission is to achieve, in partnership with departments, the highest standards of performance, efficiency and effectiveness in the civil service.

In order to achieve its objective of improving performance, CMOD tends to focus on those at middle and senior management level whom it sees as agents of change. CMOD also has a strategy of sponsoring conferences and networks to raise awareness of and facilitate good management practice. It also provides a corporate ethos for certain types of training by delivering training courses in basic management and specialist skills to staff at middle and senior management levels.

CMOD's partnership approach is intended to act as a means of transferring the knowledge and skills needed by departments. It acts as a central resource to enable departments to develop their own training capabilities. The approach is intended to add value through a strong multiplier effect, allowing CMOD to achieve high impact through its interventions.

In the survey, several questions were asked about the relationship between departments and CMOD in the provision of support for training and development. In line with its stated role in providing a service-wide perspective on the latest trends such as SMI-related developments, 63% of departments reported that they had received timely information from CMOD to enable them to plan and organise relevant training courses. However, the survey found that over two-thirds of departments had not received guidance from CMOD on training and development best practice.

CMOD responded to these findings by pointing out that it sponsors the Departmental Training Officers Network, which acts as a forum for presenting best practice within and outside the civil service. It also provides information on specific civil service policy initiatives on a regular basis to training officers in more than 40 departments and agencies. outlines CMOD's role in sponsoring a variety of networks for key groups in the civil service. In addition, CMOD intends, in relation to the downstream output of the PMDS, to develop 'templates' to assist and guide departments in identifying and delivering responses to staff training and development needs.

It appears that, while CMOD provides support to departments on matters related to specific civil service policy initiatives, there are contrasting views on the level of support it provides in relation to best training and development practice.

In addition to its training programmes, CMOD promotes training and development through various networks of staff across the civil service. Networks such as those for Departmental Training Officers, Personnel Officers and Finance Officers are seen by CMOD as an efficient and effective way of promoting and promulgating good practice.

Their agenda is heavily job oriented. In theory they should meet every quarter but meetings tend to be irregular, depending on the time of year and the importance of the issues to be discussed. For example, networks do not usually meet during the summer months while the implementation of PMDS has given rise to more frequent meetings. At a more strategic level, the Assistant Secretary network has been particularly influential over the last decade in helping to set the change agenda for the civil service. It usually meets twice a year. Secretaries General have an annual conference in addition to the regular meetings of the SMI Implementation Group of Secretaries General.

The nearest equivalent institutions to CMOD in the UK are the Cabinet Office and the Civil Service College. The roles and functions of both UK bodies and their relationship with civil service departments are outlined.

In the UK civil service, responsibility for all aspects of training and development rests with the management of individual departments, which may outsource their training to external trainers, or use the Civil Service College. The Civil Service College is an autonomous institution which, although recently returned to the aegis of the Cabinet Office, continues to operate independently and on a commercial basis. It markets its services to both the public and private sectors and operates in full competition with other training providers in the UK. The Cabinet Office monitors civil service training and provides guidance to departments on new methods and approaches. In keeping with the general movement of responsibility from the centre to individual civil service departments, the Cabinet Office has changed its approach from that of imposing standards from the centre to supporting and encouraging best practice in partnership with departments. The change is reflected in its action to replace large volumes of regulations on training and development with a statement of policy on the matter.

Departments operate within the policy as they deem fit. The change is also reflected in the action by the Cabinet Office to promote new mechanisms of researching and promulgating best practice. These include new approaches to interdepartmental networks, the nomination of centres of leadership on specific issues and the documentation and circularisation of useful information on new developments.

Management Information

In conjunction with needs analysis, good management information helps to ensure that the benefit of training is spread evenly across the organisation, with no one group or area dominating it to the detriment of other staff or the wider objectives of the organisation. It ensures that the balance of training provided matches the requirements of the organisation and permits obvious training gaps to be identified and rectified.

The survey results indicated that 82% of departments keep individual records of all courses, seminars, conferences, etc. attended by staff. However, only half of these departments use a training database to maintain such records. A database enables management to examine systematically and regularly the training trends and patterns within their organisation.

A training database is used by 67% of departments to record qualifications held by staff while 64% use it to record staff career details. Only 29% of departments use their database to record the key strengths and/or development needs of staff.

During the course of this examination it became apparent that the training units in many departments did not have all the data required by the questionnaire used in the examination and lacked methodologies to analyse the information available.

While some departments had the systems and procedures to produce accurate information quickly, many others struggled to do so over extended periods of time.

In addition, the data produced was often inconsistent and incomplete, indicating that many departments have poor information systems an or poor supervision of data collection. These difficulties had the effect of restricting the scope of analysis of the survey data.

Since 1997, departments have been supplying data on training expenditure to CMOD and this data has been used also in this examination. Notwithstanding the poor quality of data in some instances, the information submitted by departments and by CMOD has been accepted as providing a reasonable indication of the current position of training and development across the civil service.

During the course of the examination, training officers in several departments stated that they were in the process of establishing training databases, while others were updating their existing databases to take account of issues raised in this survey. It is expected also that the introduction of the new computerised Human Resources Management System will contribute to improved management information systems for training and development.

Top Management Support

Top management support for training and development is manifest in the level of resources allocated to the area, the role and status of trainers and the expectations held about the training and development function. These expectations are reflected in their action to

- integrate training and development into the strategic planning process
- establish and periodically review training and development policies and objectives
- provide the necessary resources for training and development
- recognise and deal with their own development needs.

Other than the global target of 4% of payroll costs, little attempt is made to set and promulgate indicative training targets across the civil service. Only two departments give line managers indicative targets for their staff in terms of the number of days training per person per year and only one department analyses these figures for management information purposes.

The Department of Finance considers that the implementation of the PMDS will require a more focused response at departmental level as it will establish clearer linkages between the objectives of organisations and the training and development needs of staff.

Training units are headed by staff at middle and lower management level in most departments. Only one department has a training unit headed by a Principal Officer, that is, a person at higher management level. For the purpose of this report, lower, middle and higher management refers to the grades up to Executive Officer, Assistant Principal and Assistant Secretary, respectively. Top management includes Assistant Secretaries and Secretaries General.

It may be that individual departments have a training and development management structure most appropriate for their particular circumstances. However, the absence of higher grades in full time management of the function in many departments increases the risk of training and development being distanced from top management, thereby not receiving the same degree of attention as other functions. Departments should examine ways of ensuring that training and development receives significant attention from top management. For example, regular reports updating the activities of the training and development function should be on the agenda of top management meetings.

Conclusions

The results of the survey indicate that, despite extensive and almost mandatory reference to the issue in strategy statements and documentation on all new civil service programmes, there is a fragmented approach across the civil service to training and development. The results suggest an absence of an effective common framework for setting and implementing training and development policies and plans and may also reflect differences in the approach to training and development in individual departments.

These differences are also apparent in the resources allocated to the training function and the nature of the training provided, both of which are examined in the following chapters. The Department of Finance expects that the more strategic approach to human resource management envisaged in SMI will impact on this situation.

There appears to be a high level of support for training and development by top management in some departments, contrasting with an under-supported training function in others.

Training Resources

The achievement of value for money from training and

development activity depends on the procurement and continuing availability of adequate resources. A study of economy is concerned with the quality and cost of the resources provided.

This chapter presents the results of that part of the survey which dealt with training resources. The principal training resources are

- training expenditure
- training staff
- procurement of external resources
- training facilities.

Training Expenditure

The information available about training expenditure is very limited. Details of training expenditure over a period of years, analysed by category, were sought but most departments had difficulties in providing the information requested. The details provided indicate that trends over the past three years are very similar. As a result the analysis by category is limited to 1999 expenditure only.

Much of this variation is undoubtedly due to the differing roles and training requirements of departments. For example, Revenue has a substantial internal training function given its size and specialist needs whereas Environment can more readily avail of external generic programmes.

An active training unit will incur a certain amount of overhead costs. The average department spends 8% of its training budget on overheads but this disguises a large fluctuation in overhead costs in different departments. The three largest departments had overheads ranging from 13% to 29%. Most of the smaller departments had overheads of less than 5%. The extent of the variation in expenditure levels across categories indicates that there may be problems arising from the lack of a common definition between departments of what constitutes a particular cost, or there may be differences in approach to cost allocation and apportionment. The variation limits the usefulness of cost analysis across departments for both management and evaluators.

The variation across all expenditure headings indicates a need for a common framework among departments for recording and reporting information on training and development. The purpose of the framework is to facilitate accurate analysis across the civil service, not to constrain innovation by individual departments.

Target Expenditure on Training and Development

Although the Department of Finance stipulates that expenditure on training and development must be met from existing resources, the expenditure target of 4% of payroll costs is intended to ensure that departments devote sufficient resources to meeting their staff training and development needs.

Expenditure data collated by CMOD (Appendix D) indicate that while some departments exceeded the 3% target in 1999, others had training expenditure of less than 1% of payroll costs, the average being approximately 2%.

It is unlikely that the difficulties experienced by departments in meeting the expenditure target is caused by a lack of financial resources. The problem may relate more to the state of development of the training function within departments. The civil service culture of not approving expenditure until it is shown to be justified and absolutely necessary results in less expenditure in those departments still in the process of advancing the training and development function. However, there is a risk that the combination of funding availability, pressure to meet the training expenditure target and an underdeveloped training function which lacks clarity on outputs could lead to inappropriate or wasteful expenditure on training.

It is generally agreed that it does not necessarily follow that those departments which achieve an annual percentage target of payroll expenditure are meeting their training needs more effectively and comprehensively than those which spend less than the target. The questionable value of the payroll target as an indicator suggests the need to develop more effective indicators for monitoring progress in civil service training and development.

Training Staff

The analysis of training expenditure indicates that most spending on internal training and development consists of staff costs.

The role of training staff varies across departments from full involvement in course delivery to the administration of training delivered by external trainers. Most training staff (69%) are involved in some degree of course delivery, although these staff are located predominantly in departments which have well developed training functions.

At a full time equivalent of 76, Revenue has the largest number of training staff, of whom 59 are trainers. In addition to the central Training Unit, this figure includes a number of Revenue staff who are involved in the delivery of training at a local level on a part-time basis. These staff are not part of the central Training Unit and report through their local management structures. Revenue trainers are responsible for designing, organising and delivering most training for the department. Other departments also employ significant numbers of trainers but, in many, the training unit consists of no more than one or two staff.

Training staff in ten departments have no involvement at all in course delivery. The role of the training officer in small departments is typically administrative. He or she may spend most time organising external training, with in-house training restricted to one or two short induction programmes per year.

On average, each civil service trainer is responsible for 122 staff, but the ratio of trainers to staff varies widely between departments. For example, the Department of Agriculture, Food & Rural Development and the Department of Social, Community & Family Affairs each employ over 4,000 staff, yet in the former, 10 training staff are responsible for 440 staff each, while in the latter 54 training staff are responsible for 78 staff each. The stark contrast is partly attributable to the nature of the work, the skills needed to perform that work and the grade mix. For example, Agriculture has a large professional and technical corps while DSCFA is predominately staffed by general service grades, the majority of whom are clerical staff.

Recruitment of Training Staff

Aside from consultants employed on short term contracts, all departmental training staff come from within the civil service. Most departments (76%) assign training staff to their posts without internal competition. These assignments are made by senior managers who judge the trainers to have the necessary aptitude, communication skills and expertise to fulfil the role. Some may have previous experience in training but most are new to the task. Special training for these staff is provided by 77% of departments. Although this training is usually confined to teaching and course delivery techniques, there is increasing emphasis on the design of training programmes to meet organisational needs.

On average, 72% of civil service training staff come from

the grades of Staff Officer, Executive Officer and Higher Executive Officer. The grade of the person heading up the training function on a full time basis, particularly in the larger departments, is often indicative of the level of importance attributed to it by senior management. Of the 24 departments which responded to this part of the survey, only one, Revenue, has a training function headed on a full time basis by a Principal Officer.

In over 50% of departments, the most senior person working full time in the training function is at the grade of Higher Executive Officer.

The recruitment of trainers from within the civil service has the advantage of minimising internal human resource staffing and recruitment costs. As the majority of trainers are drawn from the lower management grades of the civil service, the human resource cost of internal training is kept to the salary level of these grades. However, the value may be offset by the extent of reliance on external consultants and trainers who are priced at full market rates.

According to training theory, training should be close to its application, be consistent with the individual's value system and be integrated into the work processes and operations of the organisation. Some training specialists argue that, in the future, training will be delivered by line managers rather than by dedicated training staff or external consultants. Training staff recruited from within the civil service are in a good position to ensure these criteria are met as most are drawn from the department's line management structure.

The internal appointment system means that there is little direct experience or practical transfer of private sector training practice from outside the civil service. It is not a requirement for appointment as a trainer that a person has a training qualification. The absence of competition would indicate that, as a rule, there is no testing for relevant skills or competencies among trainers. However, on appointment, most departments send their trainers to specialist training courses, usually those conducted by the Institute of Public Administration (IPA) or the Irish Management Institute (IMI). Both organisations incorporate best practice from the public and private sectors in their programmes for trainers. There are also opportunities for learning and skills transfers from consultants and external trainers engaged by departments.

Although the departments questioned on the subject indicated they were satisfied with the quality of training provided by their training staff, only basic training evaluation systems are in use and there is no evidence that departmental trainers are using outsourced training to benchmark their own performance.

All 28 departments which replied to the survey outsource some or all of their training and development activities to external providers. In most cases (68%) they do so to compensate for the lack of relevant in-house training skills or a lack of internal resources. External training is provided by external consultants contracted to deliver specific training within the department, or on their own premises and by generic training courses offered by external training bodies.

The amount of training outsourced varies from one department to another. For example, Revenue spends 12% of its training budget on external consultants and external training courses, whereas the Department of the Environment and Local Government spends 68% of its budget on these items. Other departments which list external training courses and consultants as their most significant budgetary item include the Department of the Taoiseach (52%), the Valuation Office (55%), the Office of the Comptroller and Auditor General (57%) and the Central

Statistics Office (48 The significant differences among departments in the volume of external training reflects a number of variables, including the demand for specialist training and the availability of training staff within departments to deliver internal training.

The percentage of the average civil service training budget devoted to external training courses is 24%. External consultants and professional and academic fee refunds amount to a further 23% and 11% respectively of the average budget.

Some departments outsource training as a matter of policy. In some cases, external trainers provide all training. However, only a minority of departments (29%) negotiate a fixed rate contract with their external trainer. Given the extent of reliance on external trainers, there may be scope for cost savings in the greater use of such contracts by individual departments, or in co-operative arrangements between departments with similar training requirements.

While 86% of departments receive feedback from staff who attend external training courses, these assessments tend to be in the form of assessment sheets which are filled in immediately at the end of the course. There is little evidence of departments carrying out formal performance reviews which would provide objective information on whether staff and organisational needs are being met and performance improved through the use of external training. The lack of performance review could lead to a failure to detect poor quality external training.

Sharing Information on Generic Training

Although staff in many departments have training needs specific to their own functions, there is a significant amount of generic training which is common to most departments, for example, training in PC-based software packages such as word processing and spreadsheets and soft skills training such as customer care.

Training officers in each department negotiate separately on the price for each training programme provided by external trainers. In practice, individual departments negotiate the best deal they can, based on the number of their staff who require training. There is a risk that departments employing external trainers are unable to take advantage of the economy of scale which a body the size of the civil service should be able to negotiate.

Because they operate in isolation, training officers in individual departments may lack the information necessary to appraise critically the cost and quality of training services offered by external providers, especially in highly innovative areas such as IT.

A survey of departments for this examination in relation to external word processing and spreadsheet courses indicated that course costs in 1999 ranged from £35 to £56 per person per day. In addition, companies offering these courses usually have a fixed daily charge. Therefore, if a department is not in a position to send a full complement of staff on the course, it is not cost efficient. For example, one department needed to send staff on an advanced word processing course at a cost of £400. Although the course had room for eight people, the department was only in a position to send three. This illustrates the potential value of co-operation between departments in such circumstances.

Departments are best suited to identifying their own needs and procuring the services needed to meet those needs. However, a mechanism for centralised exchange of information would assist training officers to compare course cost and content with that being offered across the civil service. The Department of Finance considers that the Departmental Training Officers Network offers a mechanism for exchange of such information.

However, it may be that a more active approach is required. To be effective, one body should collect, analyse, store and promote training information on behalf of departments. In addition to providing benchmark information on costs and quality, this body could actively facilitate co-operation between departments on course delivery, enabling departments, especially smaller departments, to take advantage of civil service economies of scale.

This type of approach is beyond the capacity of a network and would appear to fit best within CMOD, which already undertakes the role to some extent. However, CMOD points out that collecting, analysing, storing and promoting information on training costs and quality as proposed would rely heavily on departments maintaining the necessary records.

Training Facilities

In 71% of departments surveyed, a lack of training resources, including facilities, was quoted as the primary reason for outsourcing training and development. Training facilities include accommodation, materials and equipment.

A large minority of departments surveyed (41%) have access to a departmental training centre and most (61%) hold their training courses in dedicated training rooms. Departments make use of other accommodation such as meeting rooms and conference rooms (64%), hotels (64%) and the premises of external training organisations (75%). The extent to which most departments use conference rooms and hotels indicates a general shortage of facilities and the premium placed on accommodation generally in the civil service.

A number of departments surveyed (32%) are in a position to offer training facilities to other departments but only 18% of departments state that they do so.

The results suggest that there are opportunities for cutting costs through sharing accommodation between departments. The small number of departments involved in sharing facilities indicates a lack of co-operation or co-ordination between departments on the question of accommodation.

Although hotel rooms and the premises of training companies are expensive, their use is justified in certain circumstances, as part of a planned training programme. If, as the survey suggests, the shortage in training facilities has forced departments to seek recourse to hotels for programmes which would otherwise be conducted in the department's own premises, the increased expenditure represents a lack of economy which should be addressed in the medium term.

Training in the Three Largest Departments

Revenue, Agriculture and DSCFA are the three largest departments and employ 64% of the total staff of the departments surveyed during the examination. The extent of variation between them in their training expenditure and staffing levels is illustrated in Table 3.1. Revenue has the largest training function in terms of the combination of expenditure and the number of trainers and administrative support staff, followed closely by DSCFA, with Agriculture a distant third.

A high proportion of training in all three departments is provided internally, in contrast with the amount spent by some smaller departments on external trainers. The low volume of external training may arise from limited overall training, as appears to be the case in Agriculture, or because the numbers of internal trainers and their expertise are sufficient to cover most training requirements.

There are significant differences in the absolute level of expenditure between the departments, especially Agriculture at just over 1% of payroll. However, two of the departments will have to increase their expenditure significantly, if they are to achieve the new target of 4% of payroll costs. In order to do so usefully and minimise the risk of wasteful expenditure they, like all departments, will have to match the existing quantitative measures for training with qualitative measures.

Notwithstanding the use of payroll for benchmarking purposes, there does not appear to be a common model for calculating the investment in civil service training and development. Revenue argues that, if it is intended to reflect the full cost of training as a percentage of payroll, the cost of trainee time must be included as representing the value of work forgone. There is some debate internationally in relation to the inclusion of trainee time as a training cost. Revenue appears to be the only civil service department doing so. Under this model, Revenue's training expenditure for 1999 amounted to £5.4 million, or 4% of payroll. The difference between this and the expenditure data in Table 3.1 illustrates the importance of agreeing a common model for calculating the investment in civil service training and development.

Conclusions

Although there is scope for cost savings in greater co-operation between departments and scope to improve quality in better evaluation and information sharing, the potential of these options is difficult to estimate. In general, civil service training and development is delivered economically in terms of cost but, in many departments, the economy appears to have resulted from a low level of expenditure and activity in this area. However, the examination noted several instances of good practice in civil service training and development and these are illustrated by the examples included in this report.

There are significant variations between departments in the volume and use of resources and in the training and development outputs being provided. While variation in approach to resource management is understandable, given the different nature of the work of departments, it is difficult to assess whether the extent of the variation is appropriate. The level of variation is appropriate if it results from the prioritisation of training needs and from local initiatives based on sound training and development policy to improve performance, but not appropriate if based on an *ad hoc* approach to meeting training targets.

The management of training and development is likely to come into sharp focus after the introduction of the PMDS, when demand for training output is likely to increase significantly on foot of the identification of skills gaps and the anxiety of staff and managers to acquire the necessary competencies to bridge these gaps in order to meet performance criteria.

Any increase in demand for training output is likely to stretch the capacity of those departments already struggling to meet existing targets. The introduction of the PMDS will, therefore, place a premium on the innovative management of training and development across the civil service.

Training Outputs

This chapter is concerned with issues of efficiency in the performance of training and development activities. The outputs from training and development are studied from the perspective of who receives the training and the nature of the courses provided.

The information in this chapter is based on survey responses from 21 departments. The practices of the three largest departments are highlighted.

Comparisons are also made with good practice observed in the private sector and with practice in the UK.

Who is Trained?

The situation is somewhat different at the very top and bottom of the civil service. Of the departments which responded to the survey, some had no training recorded for Secretaries General and Deputy Secretaries, with the remainder reporting only minimum training for these grades. However, the Department of Finance notes that staff serving at this level regularly attend seminars and conferences, which are considered to be important training events for top management. The survey data indicates that this form of top management training is not being recorded consistently by departments. Services staff are in the lowest grades within the civil service and the survey indicates that they receive the least training.

Informal or on-the-job training is in widespread use across departments and is often the principal means of skilling and developing staff. However, it is not recorded or monitored by departments and was, consequently, not included in this study. In a recent survey by IBEC, companies were able to report that just less than 50% of their training was provided informally, suggesting that the importance of such training has been recognised and is actively managed in the private sector.

The average number of formal training days per member of staff is a primary indicator of training performance. This average for the 21 departments surveyed is 3.3 days per year, varying from over 5 days in Health and the CSO to less than 1 day in the DPP's Office. By comparison, a recent survey of Irish company training by IBEC found that companies provide an annual average of 5.1 (2.7 formal, 2.4 informal) training days per employee per year. Some 18% of companies provided over 10 days (formal and informal) training per annum. The results suggest that the average amount of formal training provided by departments compares well with that provided by Irish companies.

However, the amount of training that a civil servant can expect depends greatly on the department in which the person is employed. The figures for the departments with the highest and lowest training days per staff member.

They indicate that the average staff member in Health or CSO receives six times more training than his or her counterpart in the DPP's Office. As training programmes frequently last for two or more days, the figures suggest that in any year, some staff in departments with the lowest average training days do not receive any training.

Cancellations

One source of inefficiency is the number of staff who put in a late cancellation for places booked on training programmes events or who fail to attend courses for which they were nominated. One in every four departments was obliged to cancel at least one training course in 1999 due to late cancellations by staff while many other courses proceeded with less than the full complement of trainees for the same reason.

The survey revealed that only three departments have a policy with regard to staff cancellation and none have a policy of penalties for late cancellations. Only 43% of departments keep records of the number of participants who cancelled or failed to attend courses for which they were nominated.

Anecdotal evidence suggests that most cancellations arise from pressure of work. This highlights time constraint as an important impediment to training. As the level of training increases in departments to meet the SMI target, management, particularly line managers, will have to develop a means of accommodating those who are required to participate in training while coping with substantial absences from work.

Top Management Training and Development

Because of the significant impact they exert on the organisation, the development of senior leaders in the leading edge companies reviewed for this study is seen as a critical training and development activity. In line with succession planning for key management positions, all of the companies reviewed have executive development programmes, often monitored separately at corporate level. These programmes are focused on developing current senior leaders and equipping those of high potential with the skills and competencies to take senior positions in the future.

Executive development programmes are typically focused on a range of areas combining strategic thinking, change management, leadership and interpersonal skills.

They are accompanied by a range of personal assessment tools, including specialised tests, assessments against the behavioural competencies and values of the organisation and ongoing coaching and mentoring of the individuals concerned.

One of the major initiatives in civil service top management training and development has been the introduction of a management development programme for Assistant Secretaries in the form of a masters degree in strategic management. The programme is run by the School of Business Studies in Trinity College on behalf of the civil service. It is designed specifically to enhance the capability of Assistant Secretaries to meet the management and policy challenges confronting the civil service. Particular emphasis is placed on policy formation and implementation, strategic management, organisation development, quantitative methods, public sector business functions and practices. The programme also covers the area of self-development.

Participants are selected competitively and the programme is run on a part-time release basis over a two year period. Since its inception in 1993, 37 Assistant Secretaries have taken part in the programme, at a cost of £534,000. This figure includes £17,800 for programme enhancement and development and £86,200 in contributions to the cost of group projects carried out as part of the programme.

Thirteen Assistant Secretaries will be commencing the 2001-2 programme shortly.

Participants on the course are required to undertake an international benchmarking study. The study produced by the class of 1993/94 on Strategic Management in the Civil Service was influential in the development of the current SMI reform programme.

The effect of the masters degree programme is to increase the average number of training days in 1999 for Assistant Secretaries across the civil service from 1.4 days to 3.6 days. The effect is more pronounced in the three largest departments. In Revenue, Agriculture and DSCFA, attendance on the course increased the number of average training days for Assistant Secretaries by 5.5 days, 3.6 days and 7.2 days, respectively. The masters programme is a valuable and highly innovative component in top management training and development. It is, however, limited to a small number of Assistant Secretaries and cannot substitute for a general programme designed to support the day to day work of all members of the civil service top management.

CMOD considers that the networks for senior managers are significant from a management development perspective. The Secretaries General have an annual conference which, in addition to the regular meetings of the SMI Implementation Group of Secretaries General, provides opportunities for discussion and exchanges on a range of issues and developments.

Time constraint, rather than budget constraint, was considered the main reason why top level civil servants in the UK underwent less training than other staff. It seems reasonable to conclude that the same constraint now applies to senior management within the Irish civil service.

In response, the UK civil service has formulated specific policies for top management training and development, part of which requires that the top 600 civil servants receive up to six weeks special training at the Civil Service College. It is expected that greater recourse to formal training and development programmes for senior management within the Irish civil service will result from the PMDS.

Training and development of senior management within the civil service needs to be focused. It should be planned, implemented and evaluated independently of general training activities. The administration and management of this area should be set up to suit the particular circumstances of top managers. Its design should be directed towards development rather than training and be strictly focused on the needs of the recipients.

Nature of Training Provided

Some indication of the relevance of training activity and the relative importance attaching to the different types of training can be obtained from considering the nature of the training courses provided. The more important areas of civil service training, as indicated by the proportion of time allocated to each, are illustrated in Figure 4.1. The information relates to internal and external training courses provided by departments. It does not include data on third level and professional education covered by the refund of fees scheme.

The figure indicates that more time is given to training which is job-specific, such as information technology (IT) training and training relevant to the functions of a department. The volume of activity in training in the SMI related areas of finance, customer care, communications and organisation driven training is markedly low.

The Department of Finance considers that the relatively low volume of activity in terms of time given to SMI related areas is a function of the extent or depth of the training required. For example, training programmes in areas such as customer care and finance are generally of a few days duration at most and training is primarily aimed at the relatively small number of officers working in these areas.

IT Training

IT training represents the largest single category of training in the civil service. This is to be expected given the level of IT development in civil service administrative processes, the constant need for skills update and the current high rate of staff turnover in the IT area.

Training time allocated to IT during 1999 was 28% for the civil service as a whole and often much higher in individual departments.

Illustrates the significant variation from the average in the amount of time allocated to IT training by individual departments. Some departments allocate over half their training time to IT. While it does not necessarily follow that other areas of training are neglected as a result, the amount of time devoted by some departments to this area does increase the risk of this happening, particularly in the absence of planning and training needs analysis.

Management Training, Seminars and Conferences

Leadership Management training takes up an average of 6% of civil service training time. This training is concentrated mainly on mid-ranking staff who may be acting as team leaders or project managers. As with other types of training, the amount of time allocated by individual departments to this area varies considerably as shown in

Attendance at seminars and conferences is on a comparable level to management training taking up, on average, approximately 6% of staff training time. Once again this figure masks wide variations in departments with one department giving over 30% of staff training time to such training events. The Department of Finance considers that seminars and conferences are important sources of leadership and management development for senior and other managers.

Function Specific Training

Function specific training refers to specialised training tailored to the specific needs of a particular job or task. Large departments with specialised areas of operations, such as Revenue, would be expected to have a considerable demand for functionspecific training illustrates the wide variation between departments in this type of training.

Foreign Language Training

Approximately 8% of staff training time is spent on foreign language training. After IT and function specific, this represents one of the largest areas of training. While the Department of Foreign Affairs estimates that it spends 15% of its training time on languages, a number of the departments surveyed reported using between 20% and 30% of their training time in this area.

Most language training is provided by the Civil Service Language Training Centre. The Centre was established to improve proficiency in EU languages, in line with Government policy. During the 1998-1999 academic year, approximately two-thirds of participants attended day classes while the remainder went to evening classes. French, German, Spanish and Italian were offered at four levels from beginners to advanced while Russian was offered at development and beginner levels only. Sign Language was offered at two levels approximating to Levels 1 and 2 of the Irish Sign Language Association.

The Centre provides document translation services and document comprehension courses to departments. Tuition in French document comprehension was provided to 60 participants in three courses during 1999. The Centre also designs and delivers one-to-one foreign language courses to officers being posted abroad or to those at the final stages of the interview procedure. Twenty such courses were provided in 1999.

There are two full-time teachers in the Language Training Centre. Other staff include additional teachers employed on a part-time basis and a clerical officer for administrative support. Expenditure on teachers salaries in the academic year September 1998 to July 1999 amounted to £200,600. This and all other costs of the Centre are borne by the Department of Finance. Departments which nominated students for evening classes paid fees of £43,800 to the Centre. Fees are not charged for day classes.

At the end of each academic year, the Centre conducts evaluations of the aural, oral and written skills of the participants. The figure for those who complete the year is derived from those who sit the evaluation. On average, just over half of those who registered attempted the evaluation, indicating a drop out rate for the 1998-99 academic year of 49%.

CMOD carried out a recent internal review of the Civil Service Language Training Centre on a one-off basis. The Centre caters for all departments but is the direct responsibility of CMOD. The result of the review is the discontinuation of language training other than French and German in order to ensure a more focused approach.

Language training is an important element of training given the role of civil servants at European level. However, Table C.2 in Appendix C indicates considerable variation in time allocated to language training between departments. For example, departments such as the Civil Service Commission and Enterprise, Trade and Employment devote over 30% of training time to this area while the Department of Tourism, Sport and Recreation did not have any language training in 1999. This finding and the drop out rate experienced by the Language Training Centre suggest that, notwithstanding the review by CMOD, departments themselves should review their language training programmes in accordance with actual needs.

Irish Language Training

Gaeleagras na Seirbhíse Poiblí (Gaeleagras) was established by the Department of Finance in 1971 with the general aim of promoting the Irish language throughout the civil service, thereby enabling departments to conduct State business through Irish. Gaeleagras fulfils this role by providing language training, proficiency testing and support to departments.

In addition to providing day and evening training courses, Gaeleagras arranges specialist courses to meet specific demands from departments. Its most popular training programmes are Gaeltacht courses which attracted 404 participants from a total of 648 people who attended Gaeleagras training in 1998-99.

Gaeleagras carries out proficiency testing on behalf of

the Civil Service Commission to assess the competency in Irish of candidates taking part in civil service competitions. Gaeleagras assumed this function in April 1999 and proficiency tests were carried out on 82 candidates that year.

In its role of supporting departments Gaeleagras provides a translation service, particularly in relation to parliamentary questions and correspondence. The volume of translation work is growing and it is taking up proportionally more of the available teaching time. Given the confidential nature of much of the material, the tight deadlines and the technical nature of the terms used, it is often not possible to outsource this work.

There are two full-time teachers in Gaeleagras with administrative support provided by one full-time and one part-time clerical officer. Other teachers are employed on a part-time basis for specific tasks. Expenditure in 1999 amounted to £162,000, excluding accommodation costs. All Gaeleagras costs are borne by the Department of Finance.

Training in the Three Largest Departments

The illustration highlights the degree of variation in approach to training taken by these departments. Even allowing for the impact of their differing operational responsibilities and administrative structures, the degree of inconsistency is unexpected and reflects the position among departments in general.

The limited nature of formal training needs analysis undertaken by the civil service indicates that demand is the main basis for deciding what type of training will be provided. While responding to demand is essential, the absence of needs analysis increases the risk that the type of training provided is inadequate and/or inappropriate.

The refund of fees scheme provides financial support and special leave for staff studying for a recognised professional, technical or third level qualification. The course must be relevant to the work of the department and expenditure under the scheme is subject to limitations imposed by each department's annual training budget. Each department has discretion, within Department of Finance guidelines, in formulating its own policy and procedures for the scheme.

Most courses are attended on a part-time, or evening basis and the results are recognised academic and professional qualifications. Third level and professional institutions provide top quality facilities and resources and offer large economies of scale, suggesting that this type of training and development can be cost effective and efficient.

Revenue was involved jointly in the design of an M.Sc. programme in Taxation with Dublin City University and the taxation profession. The programme covers knowledge of tax theory and its role in the economic, social and legal system, the practice and administration of taxation, strategic planning and management and research methodologies. The course is completed on a part-time basis over two years at a cost of £7,000. Since its inception in 1996, Revenue has sponsored sixteen of its staff on the course.

The average department spends about 11% of its total training budget on refunding fees for academic and professional courses undertaken by staff. Approximately 4% of civil servants avail of this type of training. Table 4.5 illustrates the proportion of training budget used for fee refunds in selected departments and the percentage of staff who avail of this training option.

Conclusions

The extent of the divergence in training output data

suggests that there is considerable scope for inefficiency in the provision of civil service training.

In the absence of a reliable benchmark, it is impossible to state which departments are performing well and which are not. Departments themselves do not have systems for measuring their performance in this respect. It can be stated that, on the whole, there is insufficient training being provided to the highest and lowest grades in the civil service and that certain areas of training absorb a disproportionate amount of resources while others, such as management training, may require more attention.

The fact that most training being provided at present is technical in nature would suggest that the current emphasis by departments is on training in skills and knowledge in specific areas. Training on the broader front dealing with roles, attitudes and behaviours is less in evidence. The lack of consistency across departments in this type of training suggests an absence of appreciation, at corporate and departmental level, of the value of such training and development as a means of improving performance.

Consideration should be given to the mandatory provision of training in people management skills to those newly appointed to civil service positions with staff responsibilities.

The Department of Finance considers that the introduction of the PMDS will provide a systematic means to assess, prioritise and respond to training and development needs, thus addressing the issues raised in this part of the report. However, notwithstanding the promise offered by the introduction of the PMDS, the findings of the examination indicate that there is an urgent need to review all aspects of civil service training and development output and to put in place standard systems and indicators to enable regular and independent review.

Bibliography

Abdullah, S. (1998). Helping faculty to make the paradigm shift from oncampus teaching to distance education at the Institut Teknologi Mara, Malaysia. In Latchem & Lockwood (1998) pp. 85-94.

Dillon, C., & Walsh, S. (1992). Faculty: the neglected resource in distance education. *American journal of distance education*, 6:3, 5-21.

Graham, K., & Tierney, J. (2003). *Improving teacher education through human resource development at ITEK.* Midterm review for Nuffield Foundation.

Commonwealth Programme 2001-2005. Oxford: Nuffield Foundation. Gunawardena, C., & Zittle, R (1998). Faculty development programmes in distance education in American higher education. In Latchem & Lockwood (1998) pp. 105-114.

Gunn, C., & Panko, M (1998). Staff development within a flexible and open learning course. In Latchem & Lockwood (1998) pp. 212-220.

Haag, S. (1992). Speaking personally. *American journal of distance education*, 6:3, 72-6.

Haigh, N. (1998). Staff development: an enabling role. In Latchem & Lockwood (1998) pp. 182-192.

Koul, B. (1998). Proactive staff development: the Indira

Gandhi National Open University experience. In Latchem & Lockwood (1998) pp. 75-84.

Latchem, C., and Lockwood, F. (Ed.) (1998). *Staff development in open and flexible learning*. London: Routledge.

Lentell, H. (1994). Professional development. *Open praxis*, 1994 (1), 29-30.

Lentell, H. (1996). Professional development. *Open praxis*, 1996 (1), 40-41.

Randell, C., & Blitzer, E. (1998). Staff development in support of effective student learning in South African distance education. In Latchem & Lockwood (1998) pp. 137-147.

Senkomago, N. (2003). *Teacher education at a distance: impact on community – research report from Uganda*. Cambridge: IEC.

Sewart, D. (1998). Tuition and counselling: supporting the teachers for competitive advantage. In Latchem & Lockwood (1998) pp. 148-156.

Spronk, B. (1998). Seeing the world through two pairs of eyes: staff development issues in distance/open learning programmes for First Nations peoples in Canada. In Latchem & Lockwood (1998) pp. 127- 136.

Wrightson, T. (1998). *Distance education in action: the Northern Integrated Teacher Education Project in Uganda*. Cambridge: International Extension College.

Index

GI1149